Titanic
A Very Peculiar History™

With added iceberg

'Where you go, I go.'

Ida Straus to her husband Isidor, who refused to leave the *Titanic* while younger people were still on board

For my father, who shares his love of stormy seas with anyone brave enough to sail with him.

JP

Editor: Stephen Haynes
Editorial assistants: Rob Walker, Mark Williams
Additional artwork: Mark Bergin, Bill Donohoe

Published in Great Britain in MMXII by
Book House, an imprint of
The Salariya Book Company Ltd
25 Marlborough Place, Brighton BN1 1UB
www.salariya.com
www.book-house.co.uk

HB ISBN-13: 978-1-907184-87-1

1 3 5 7 9 8 6 4 2

A CIP catalogue record for this book is available from the British Library.

Printed and bound in Dubai.

Printed on paper from sustainable sources.

Titanic
A Very Peculiar History™

With added iceberg

D ... n

'We have arrived at a new time – and with this new time, strange methods, huge forces and combinations – a *Titanic* world – have spread all around us.'

Winston Churchill, speaking in 1909

'The science of shipbuilding has now reached a degree of perfection [that] has not only robbed the sea of its terrors, but has imposed upon its unstable surface comforts, and even luxuries, of travel surpassing anything on land.'

Belfast News-Letter, 21 October 1910

'I cannot imagine any condition which would cause a modern ship to founder... Shipbuilding has gone beyond that...'

Captain Edward Smith, six years before the maiden voyage of the *Titanic*

'To call this ship unsinkable is flying in the face of God!'

Mrs Esther Hart , passenger

Contents

Sent to Davy Jones's Locker

The story that is about to unfold may be the most famous maritime disaster in history, but it's just one of a long list of horrifying incidents. When things go wrong at sea, they go very badly wrong. No wonder sailors of old believed in Davy Jones, a demon who rules over the evil spirits of the deep...

• Bad navigation
On the night of 22 October 1707, a Royal Navy fleet returning from Gibraltar to Portsmouth sailed through dangerous reefs off the Isles of Scilly. Four ships – HMS *Association*, *Eagle*, *Romney* and *Firebrand* – sank, and over 1,500 sailors died, their bodies washing up on shore for days afterward. An investigation found that the main reason for the disaster was navigational error, and a prize was set up to find a better way to calculate longitude (a ship's east-west position).[1]

• Short cut
Bound for Jakarta in Indonesia, the *Tek Sing* left the port of Amoy (now Xiamen in Fujian, China) packed with porcelain and Chinese emigrants. A month into the voyage, the captain, Io Tauko, decided to chance a short cut through the Gaspar Strait. On 6 February 1822 the *Tek Sing* struck a reef and sank within the hour, in about 30 metres of water. Around 1,600 people went down with the ship.

1. It was won in 1765 by Yorkshire clockmaker John Harrison.

• Fire

On 15 June 1904 the paddle-steamer *General Slocum* caught fire in New York's East River. All told, more than 1,000 people died – mostly women and children on their way to a picnic – making it New York's worst disaster until the 9/11 attacks in 2001. It was later found that the firm that made the lifejackets had filled them with cheap, useless material instead of cork, then added iron bars to make them the correct weight! Anyone who strapped on one of these jackets and jumped into the water quickly sank to the bottom.

• Typhoon

The Japanese steamship SS *Kiche Maru* sank during a typhoon in the Pacific Ocean on 22 September 1912. More than 1,000 people lost their lives. As there were no survivors, very little is known about what actually happened. The storm sank hundreds of vessels and devastated the ports of Osaka and Nagoya.

• Torpedoed

The liner RMS *Lusitania* was torpedoed without warning by a German U-boat (submarine) on 7 May 1915 and sank in 18 minutes off the southwest coast of Ireland. Two explosions rocked the ship. The first was caused by the torpedo, but a second, much larger explosion has never been fully explained – was the *Lusitania* secretly carrying armaments? An estimated 1,198 people died, including 139 US citizens, and the attack eventually led to the United States declaring war on Germany.

• **Fog**

The French steamer *La Bourgogne* sank on 4 July 1898 after the British sailing ship *Cromartyshire* accidentally rammed her in dense fog off Cape Sable, Nova Scotia; 565 lives were lost. Survivors described brutal scenes as the crew of the French ship grabbed all available lifeboats and rafts. Panic broke out, passengers using knives and revolvers in a mad rush to recapture the lifeboats.

• **Snow**

On 24 March 1878 the training vessel HMS *Eurydice* was caught in a heavy snowstorm off the Isle of Wight. The sailing ship capsized and sank, and those who survived the sinking soon froze to death in the icy waters. Just two of the ship's 366 crew and trainees survived.

• **Overloading**

The paddle-steamer *Brother Jonathan* sank off Crescent City, California on 30 July 1865. Even before passengers got on, the captain had noticed the ship lying dangerously low in the water, but kept schtum after being threatened with the sack. Dock hands then loaded a giant ore crusher onto a part of the hull that had only just been patched up. Encountering stormy weather, the captain headed for safety. The ship had almost made it to port when a large wave drove it onto an uncharted rock, ripping a huge hole in the hull. Soon after, the ore crusher crashed through the weakened hull. A single lifeboat escaped carrying 19 people, but 225 others died in the wreck.

• **Burst boiler**

In April 1865 the American Civil War had just ended, and the Mississippi riverboat SS *Sultana* was carrying thousands of former Union prisoners of war back north. At about 2.00 a.m. on the 27th the boilers exploded, breaking the ship in half. The explosion killed many passengers and threw others hundreds of feet into the water. A few survivors were plucked from trees along the riverbank, but many of the soldiers couldn't swim, and an estimated 1,500–1,900 people died.

• **Sharks, salt and thirst**

On 30 July 1945 the USS *Indianapolis* was torpedoed by a Japanese submarine and sank in 12 minutes. Around 300 crew members went down with the ship. The remaining 880 floated in the water, waiting for help. But the US Navy did not know about the sinking for another four days. By then, hundreds more had died from cold, lack of food and water, salt poisoning and shark attacks. Only 317 survived out of 1,196 crew – the greatest single loss of life at sea in the history of the US Navy.

• **Collision**

Sailing from Samar Island in the Philippines to the capital, Manila, the passenger ferry MV *Doña Paz* collided with a tanker carrying 8,800 barrels of oil products on 20 December 1987. A giant ball of fire immediately engulfed both ships. The *Doña Paz* sank within two minutes and over 4,380 people died – the greatest loss from a single ship in peacetime.

Give me your
tired, your poor,
Your huddled
masses...

INTRODUCTION

A perilous journey

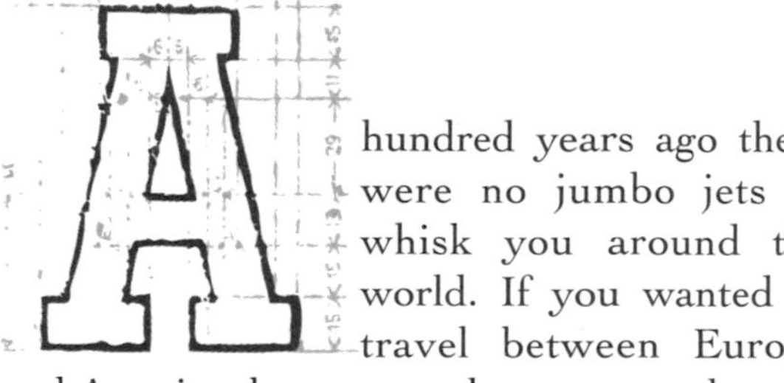

A hundred years ago there were no jumbo jets to whisk you around the world. If you wanted to travel between Europe and America there was only one way – by sea.

During the 19th century it took sailing ships weeks, if not months, to complete the often hazardous crossing of the vast Atlantic Ocean. Many vessels were small, cramped and uncomfortable, and both passengers and crew suffered horribly.

If, like me, you're the sort of person who gets seasick sitting in a rubber dinghy, just imagine what it was like being tossed around by stormy seas for weeks on end. At the beginning of the voyage there was usually a desperate scramble to get one of the top bunks – to avoid a veritable Niagara of vomit from the seasick passengers above. Home comforts? Forget it! Many ships carrying livestock were simply hosed out for the return trip with immigrant traffic, earning them the nickname 'cattle boats'.

Though terrifying tempests are two a penny on the Atlantic, safety wasn't a major concern for shipowners and many vessels were lost without trace. Yet despite the horrors at sea, countless thousands of Europeans were willing to risk the journey to begin a new life in America. Some were escaping from poverty, religious persecution or war. Others simply hoped for a more prosperous life in fast-growing US cities such as New York. The stampede to find gold in California in 1849 and northern Canada in 1896 also lured thousands hoping to strike it lucky.

The 'bowl of tears'

From the mid-1840s onwards, over a million people fled from starvation as the Great Famine devastated Ireland. Shady shippers ferried them in the holds of rotting, leaky vessels totally unsuited to the rough crossing. So many died, mostly from cholera and typhoid, that the Atlantic became known as the 'bowl of tears'.

- Onboard fires killed over 9,000 people. The *Ocean Monarch* caught fire on 24 August 1848, just 40 km out of Liverpool. Many passengers had to jump into the sea and drifted out of sight on the tide. Though two ships were nearby to help, 170 victims died.

- Between 1845 and 1849, 50 ships sank after hitting icebergs or rocks. When, on 29 April 1849, the *Hannah* struck an iceberg around 4.00 a.m., the crew jumped into a lifeboat and rowed off, leaving the passengers to die. But the ship took 40 minutes to sink, giving the passengers time to climb onto the iceberg. They huddled together in their nightshirts for 15 hours until another ship came to the rescue. Though 129 were saved, many others were crushed, drowned or frozen to death.

- In a bad storm, the captain of the *Londonderry* forced all 174 passengers into one small cabin. When the door was opened the next morning, 21 women, 23 men and 28 children were found crushed or suffocated.

Mercifully, by the late 1840s, crossings became faster, safer and more reliable with the arrival of steamships. These ships were much bigger than the old wooden sailing vessels and weren't at the mercy of the winds. A typical crossing now took just two weeks.

While most passengers still travelled in third class on the lower decks, more and more wealthy Europeans wanted to visit America, a mecca for money-makers. At the same time, rich Americans were drawn to stylish European cities like Paris, London and Rome, and fabulous holiday destinations such as the French Riviera and the pyramids of Egypt. These passengers wanted luxury, and they were willing to pay top dollar for it. They travelled in first-class cabins on upper decks, while those who wanted a reasonable level of comfort at a more affordable price travelled in second class.

By the end of the 19th century, dozens of luxurious ocean liners plied the Atlantic route from Europe to America and back. An unofficial award, known as the Blue Riband, was given to the ship that made the fastest crossing. In the 1890s the Cunard and White Star lines battled tooth and nail to win the award, as making the fastest crossing was seen as the best way to win customers. Then both lines were blown away by German-built speedsters such as the *Deutschland*, launched in 1900, which set a record-breaking speed of 23 knots (42.71 km/h).

Breaking records was all well and good, but the *Deutschland*'s engines vibrated so badly that she was nicknamed the 'cocktail shaker'. As a result, part of the ship's stern even dropped off in 1902! But national pride was at stake, so Cunard built two fast new liners, *Lusitania* and *Mauretania*, that would win back the Blue Riband for Britain. Meanwhile, the White Star Line dropped out of the competition. Why? Its boss, J. Bruce Ismay, realised that passengers preferred comfort over speed, even if it meant spending an extra day at sea. He planned to build three gigantic liners that were going to be bigger and more lavish than anything else afloat. One of the three, the *Titanic*, was destined to become the most famous ship since Noah's Ark – but for all the wrong reasons.

Bigger, faster, grander

Thanks to the latest technology and fierce competition for passengers, transatlantic liners changed dramatically in the 70 years or so before the *Titanic* was launched.

- In 1837 the paddle-steamer SS *Great Western* (designed by the famous railway engineer Isambard Kingdom Brunel) made her first Atlantic crossing. It took 15 days, compared with two months by sailing ships.

- In 1840 the Cunard Line built four slightly smaller copies of the *Great Western*. One of these, the *Britannia*, became the Cunard's first regular passenger steamship, sailing from Liverpool to Boston.

- In 1847 Brunel's SS *Great Britain* became the first iron-hulled, screw-driven ship to cross the Atlantic. More efficient propellers now began to replace the paddle-wheels used by earlier ocean liners.

- In 1858 the launch of Brunel's SS *Great Eastern* heralded the era of the superliners. Five times bigger than any previous vessel, she remained the largest ship in the world for over 40 years. Driven by a combination of sails, paddles and a propeller, she could carry 4,000 passengers around the world – without needing to stop for fuel. She was supersafe, too – the first iron ship with a double hull all

Great Eastern 1858

the way from the waterline to the keel, and with 16 watertight compartments. These features saved her from disaster in 1862 when she scraped a rock and opened up a gash in her side over 25 m long and 2.7 m wide.

- In 1870, White Star Line's RMS *Oceanic* set a new standard for luxury on the ocean waves. First-class cabins were placed amidships (in the middle of the ship), away from the vibration of the engines and with the least ocean movement. Extra-large portholes provided more light, while most first-class cabins also had running water and electric bells to summon a steward. Happy days!

- In the 1880s ocean liners got bigger to ferry a new flood of emigrants to the United States and Australia. However, to save on coal, two of the largest liners, the *Umbria* and her sister ship the *Etruria*, were still fitted with sails (they were the last such vessels).

They have to share a bathroom, though, poor things!

Interior of a first-class cabin

Titanic was a home from home for the cream of British and American society

Chapter One

A Floating Marvel

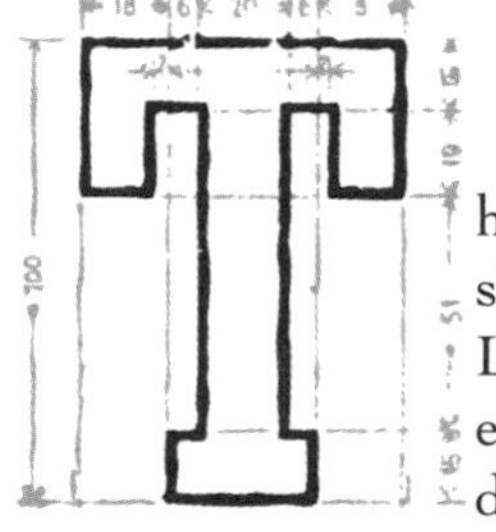

The *Titanic* and her two sister ships were born in London on a still summer's evening in 1907, during a dinner party held at the London mansion of Lord William James Pirrie, head of Harland & Wolff, the famous shipbuilders of Belfast in Ireland.[1] Among the guests were J. Bruce Ismay, managing director of the White Star Line, and his wife Florence. Though Harland & Wolff had a

1. now Northern Ireland. Twelve times in the previous 20 years, Harland & Wolff had built more ships than any other shipyard in the world. In 1912 the firm was again top of the table.

reputation as the finest shipbuilders in the world, Lord Pirrie hadn't been getting much sleep recently. His main client, the White Star Line, was in danger of being upstaged by its arch-rival, the Cunard Line. Cunard's speedy new liner, the *Lusitania*, was expected to smash the record for the fastest Atlantic crossing.

But Ismay had thought of a clever wheeze: the White Star Line would build the biggest ships ever to set sail across the Atlantic, with all the comfort and elegance of the world's finest hotels. Their supreme luxury would seduce wealthy customers, while their size would allow them to pack in more second- and third-class passengers on each crossing.

Over cigars and brandy, the two men hatched a plan to build two monster liners. At 45,000 tonnes, each would be one and a half times the size of Cunard's biggest ships – and the largest man-made objects ever built. Grand ships needed grand names: *Olympic* and *Titanic*. And if successful, a third would follow, the *Gigantic* (later renamed *Britannic*). J. Pierpont Morgan, White Star's owner, quickly agreed. He could hear the cash tills ringing already.

The White Star Line

Meet the team that dreamed up the *Titanic*:

- **Full name:** Oceanic Steam Navigation Company or White Star Line of Boston Packets.
- **Owner:** American railroad, coal and steel magnate John Pierpont Morgan. His firm, International Mercantile Marine (IMM), stumped up the money to build the *Titanic* and her two sister ships.
- **Managing Director:** Joseph Bruce Ismay (since 1899).
- **Origins:** White Star switched from mining Australian goldfields to luxury shipping after Thomas Henry Ismay (Joseph's father) bought the bankrupt company in 1867 for the knockdown price of £1,000.
- **Shipbuilder:** Harland & Wolff. Liverpool merchant Gustav Wolff approached Ismay during a game of billiards and offered to finance the new shipping line if his Belfast shipyard, Harland & Wolff, built the ships to its own design (with no expense spared). The first orders were placed in 1869. Harland & Wolff agreed not to build any vessels for White Star's rivals, provided White Star didn't use any other shipbuilders.
- **First ships:** White Star splashed out on six ships of the *Oceanic* class: *Oceanic*, *Atlantic*,

Baltic and *Republic*, followed by the slightly larger *Celtic* and *Adriatic*.

- **Routes:** At first White Star ships plied Australian routes, but in 1871 the line began its first Atlantic service between New York and Liverpool (with a call at Queenstown, now Cobh, in Ireland). Rivals really sat up and took notice in 1873, when the *Baltic* set a new speed record for crossing the Atlantic.

- **Main competitor:** The Cunard Line, set up in 1839 by Samuel Cunard. To cut competition, J. P. Morgan had already snapped up many of White Star's smaller rivals.

What's in a name?

- Ships built by the White Star Line generally had names ending in *-ic*, such as *Oceanic*, *Baltic* or *Majestic*, while the rival Cunard Line had names ending in *-ia*, like *Lusitania*.

- The names *Olympic* and *Titanic* were chosen to emphasise how vast these ships were compared to their rivals.

- *Titanic* was named after a race of giants from Greek mythology. The Titans fought a war against the Greek gods led by Zeus – and lost. Many had a very unpleasant fate. For example, Atlas was condemned by Zeus to stand at the western edge of the world for eternity and hold up the sky on his shoulders.

When he returned to Belfast, Pirrie gathered together his key staff, among them his nephew Thomas Andrews, Harland & Wolff's innovative chief designer.[2] Andrews and his deputy Edward Wilding spent months preparing the designs, helped by a team of architects and draftsmen. In a world without computers, this meant countless hours of calculating, sketching ideas and drafting minutely detailed drawings by hand. The men worked tirelessly, however, and by the summer of 1908 the plans were ready.

Andrews knew that Ismay cared more about comfort than speed, and at a slower pace passengers would enjoy a smoother ride as the engines vibrated less. The superliners were also to be fitted with the latest safety devices. The hull had a double bottom divided into 16 compartments, each of which could be isolated by electric watertight doors. According to an article in the respected *Shipbuilder* magazine, published in 1911, these would make the *Titanic* and her sister ships 'practically

2. Andrews had a reputation as a workaholic, often arriving at the shipyard at 4.00 a.m. in a paint-smeared bowler hat and with his jacket pockets stuffed with plans and sketches.

unsinkable',[3] as they could limp back to port even if three or four compartments in the bow were flooded.

So preparations went ahead for building the enormous ships at Harland & Wolff's Queen's Island shipyard in Belfast. Meanwhile, on the other side of the Atlantic, Ismay was in talks with the New York Harbor Board. White Star needed to extend the piers there so they would be long enough for the new superliners.[4]

On 16 December 1908 the first keel section of the *Olympic* was laid down on Slip No. 2, and some three months later a second keel was laid down for *Titanic*[5] on Slip No. 3. The two sister ships were built side by side, and though the *Titanic* is far more famous today, at the time the *Olympic* hogged the headlines as she was the first to be built.[6]

3. This phrase may have been lifted from a publicity brochure produced by White Star in 1910, which claimed the two ships were 'designed to be unsinkable'.
4. After pressure from J. Pierpont Morgan, the piers were built at the city's expense, much to the annoyance of many local taxpayers.
5. Originally known only as 'Order No. 401'.
6. As the lead ship, Olympic*'s hull was painted light grey to make it show up better in photographs of the launch.* Titanic*'s was not, nor were so many pictures taken by Harland & Wolff of her construction and launch.*

Ready, steady, spend!

How do you build the world's largest liner? Think big and spend like crazy!

- None of the existing slipways at Harland & Wolff were big enough, so three of the old berths were combined into two huge new slips. To take the weight of the giant hull, wooden piles were sunk deep into the ground and covered in a layer of concrete 1.4 m thick.
- Two superheavy mooring poles were also erected at the new wharf.
- An enormous new metal framework was built over the two slipways at a cost of £100,000. Known as the Great Gantry, it was equipped with a series of ten cranes and four large electric lifts that could raise workers and materials onto the highest decks of the two ships. Together the structure and its equipment weighed a hefty 6,000 tonnes and towered 69 m over the dock.
- The latest hi-tech machinery was brought in to prepare the giant steelwork of the two ships.
- A 200-tonne floating crane costing £30,000 was bought from the Benrather Company in Germany to lift engines, boilers and funnels into the finished hulls at the outfitting wharf after the launch.

- In March 1911 the Belfast Harbour Commissioners also finished building a vast new dry dock, the largest in the world. Named the Thompson Graving Dock, it cost £350,000 to build.

- A new road, lit by electric lamps, had to be strong enough to support trams carrying loads of up to 150 tonnes.

- New dry and wet docks were also built in Southampton harbour (the departure point for the transatlantic service) to fit the floating leviathans.

- By the time the *Titanic* was built, the wage bill at the Harland & Wolff shipyard was £25,000 a week, a huge figure for the time.

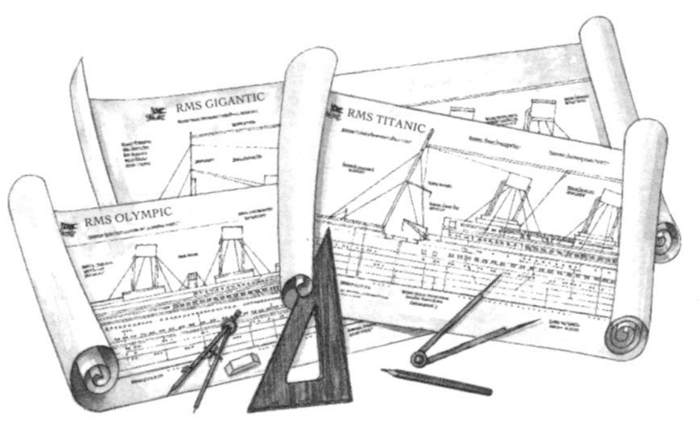

Within a few months the skeleton of the *Titanic* took shape. The keel was like a long backbone, while a giant steel frame of beams and girders acted as the ribcage. The frame was then clad in a skin of 2,000 overlapping steel plates.[7] The whole structure was held together by millions of rivets. Where possible, 7-tonne hydraulic machines were used to rivet the steel sections together, but many were put in by hand. Imagine the din as gangs of men hammered away, sections of steel clanged together and machines rattled and whirred.[8]

White Star gave Harland & Wolff complete freedom to build the very best ships they could – the shipyard workers used steel of 'battleship quality'. For over two years, thousands worked from 7.50 a.m. to 5.30 p.m., five days a week (plus a half-day on Saturday), to build the *Titanic* and her sister ship the *Olympic*. All of Belfast watched in awe as the two gargantuan ships rose high above the city.

7. Most of the steel plates were 2.5 cm or more thick, 1.8 m wide and 9 m long. The largest were 11 m long and weighed 41 tonnes.
8. The noise was so loud that workers could not hear each other speak. Recent studies show that working in a very noisy environment not only causes deafness, but can also affect workers' balance – so it may have contributed to some of the deaths in the shipyard.

Dockyard dangers

Shipbuilding has always been a dangerous trade, but workers in the early 20th century took risks that would never be accepted today. They had little choice – in Belfast at that time, you either worked or starved. During the building of the *Titanic* there were 250 accidents. Most were caused by falls from the scaffolding around the ship.

- The Harland & Wolff directors' minute book records six deaths on the *Titanic* itself and two in the works. Compensation amounted to £1,133.

- Riveters worked in gangs of two men and a boy. Fifteen-year-old Sam Smith was a 'catchboy' – he caught the red-hot rivets in a bucket as they were thrown out of the portable furnace in which they were being cast. On 20 April 1910, the first day of work on the steel plates, he fell from planking around the hull and was killed. His father died 6 months later when a section of decking collapsed underneath him.

- A worker whose foot was crushed by a falling hoist was carried home by his mates in a wheelbarrow. Though he knew his foot was badly hurt, he refused to take his boot off. Once out of the boot, the swollen foot would never go back in – and if he didn't report for work next morning he could lose his job.

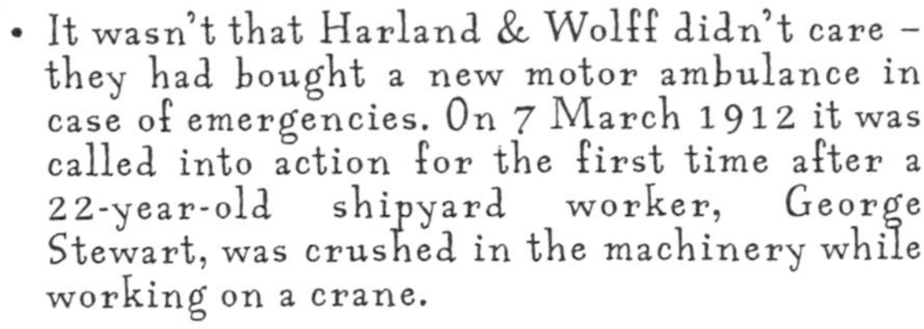

- It wasn't that Harland & Wolff didn't care – they had bought a new motor ambulance in case of emergencies. On 7 March 1912 it was called into action for the first time after a 22-year-old shipyard worker, George Stewart, was crushed in the machinery while working on a crane.

- One shipyard worker was killed during the launching ceremony. James Dobbins was knocking out supports below the hull when his foot got pinned down by one of the falling timbers, just as the massive bulk of the *Titanic* started heading down the slipway. Though he was dragged clear by his colleagues and moved to a nearby hospital, he died from his wounds later that day.

Catching rivets

The launch

The *Titanic* was launched on 31 May 1911. To attract extra publicity, the *Olympic* sailed the same day from Belfast and could be seen floating nearby. It was a warm, sunny day and some 100,000 people paid one shilling (5p) each for a ticket to cheer the launch from the dockside. Four grandstands were built for VIPs, ticket-holders and members of the press, while workers and their families found places to watch in and around the shipyard.

At this stage *Titanic* was just a massive empty shell. But at almost 25,000 tonnes, she would still be one of the heaviest movable objects in the world. Some 21 tonnes of soft soap, tallow and train oil were used to lubricate the 235 m slipway for the launch, creating a greasy coating 2.5 cm thick. Hydraulic launching rams were placed at the top of the slipway to give the ship a nudge in the right direction. Throughout the morning, the clang of hammers was heard around the dockyard as the workers prepared for the launch, most of them hidden from view.

A red launch flag was raised on *Titanic*'s stern just after noon, and a few minutes later two red rockets were fired into the sky to announce that the launch would happen shortly. Around 12.10 p.m. another rocket soared into air as a warning to other boats nearby that the giant ship was about to head down the slipway. Gangway!

Below the hull, the wooden supports were knocked free and workers scrambled for safety. Lord Pirrie gave the launch signal, the mechanical triggers were released, and at 12.13 p.m. the *Titanic* slid majestically into the water, accompanied by a great cheer. She took 62 seconds to slip down the 'ways', the wooden platforms that sloped down towards the water.

At last the *Titanic* was afloat. The crowd went mad – tugs blew their shrill sirens, women and children waved their handkerchiefs, and workmen threw their caps into the air. To celebrate the launch, Lord Pirrie entertained guests including J. Pierpont Morgan and J. Bruce Ismay at the shipyard. Meanwhile, the press was treated to a roast-beef dinner at Belfast's Grand Central Hotel (to encourage them to write good reviews!). Then at 3.00 p.m. Pirrie and Ismay sailed for Liverpool on the maiden voyage of the *Olympic*, the *Titanic*'s sister ship.

They just shoves 'er in

You may have heard a story that the *Titanic* was doomed because there was no proper naming or christening ceremony. In the 1900s a bottle of champagne was often smashed against a ship's hull to celebrate its birth and bring it luck. But Harland & Wolff never christened their ships. As one worker commented, 'They just builds 'er and shoves 'er in.' Later on, confusion over whether the ship was christened or not arose from a scene in the 1958 movie *A Night to Remember*, which borrowed footage from the launch of Cunard's *Queen Elizabeth* in 1938.

The floating giant

Everything about the *Titanic* was colossal, including the cost:

- It took 15,000 men 26 months to build the ship at a cost of £1,500,000 (a third of this was wages).
- Over 3 million rivets were used to clamp *Titanic*'s steel plates together.
- The *Titanic* was 269 m long. Stood on end, she would have been just 31 m shorter than the Eiffel Tower (300 m), at that time the world's tallest structure.
- The ship was 28 m broad – as wide as four-lane motorway.
- She was 33 m high from the keel to the top of the funnels – the same height as an 11-storey building.
- There were nine decks, lettered A to G.
- With a gross tonnage of 47,071 tonnes and a displacement of 53,149 tonnes, the *Titanic* was the world's heaviest ship and the largest machine ever built (extra cabins and extended B-deck staterooms made her heavier than the *Olympic*).
- The ship had 8 km of decks.

Titanic's rudder and propellers

- The rudder weighed more than 100 tonnes and was taller than a 5-storey building.
- The three anchors together weighed 28 tonnes (the weight of 20 cars). The central anchor alone weighed 15.5 tonnes and required a team of 20 horses to pull it.
- The ship could carry up to 2,435 passengers and 892 crew, making a total of 3,327 people on board.

Fitting out

After the launch, the *Titanic* was immediately towed by a team of tugs to Harland & Wolff's fitting-out basin. Here, over the next ten months, the empty hull was transformed into a luxury hotel by 4,000 workers on board ship and in the workshops.

There were 1,001 jobs to be done, from adding the top decks to installing the 2,000 portholes and the indoor swimming pool. Heavy machinery, such as the engines and boilers, was hoisted on board by the giant floating crane, whose two hooks could lift a weight of 200 tonnes. Then the final parts of the ship's superstructure were added, such as the officers' quarters, the gymnasium, the bridge and the four huge funnels. It took an army of joiners, painters, plumbers, electricians, tilers, carpet-layers and designers to create the legendary cabins and rooms. A 300-page book was issued as a guide to fitting and decorating the ship, with a 16-page section just on how to get the plumbing right.

The 'Millionaire's Special'

No expense was spared in the building of the *Titanic*, a fact endlessly repeated in White Star's publicity:

- *'Without doubt the finest piece of workmanship of its kind afloat':* The centrepiece of the floating hotel was the first-class staircase, 5 m wide and 20 m high, with elegantly carved banisters and elaborate ironwork. It was lit from above by a spectacular glass dome, from which hung a giant chandelier.

- *'When talk becomes monotonous... indulge here in bridge and whist or retire with a book':* What larks! The grand first-class lounge was designed to look like the palace of Versailles, with a spectacular marble fireplace and elegant statues.

- Passengers could enjoy *'something of the grandeur of the mysterious East'* in the Turkish Bath, whose cooling room looked like a Sultan's palace.

- *'Seated around the home-like fire, we may smoke and drink as wisely and well as we feel inclined':* The place to relax after dinner, the first-class smoking room (men only) was furnished like a posh London gentlemen's club with stained-glass windows and leather chairs grouped around small tables.

- The largest room on board, the first-class dining saloon, was over 30 m long and featured cosy, Jacobean-style alcoves and leaded windows. It could seat over 550 passengers at the same time.

- While waiting to take their seats in the dining saloon, parties and friends could enjoy the delights of the *'charming, sunlit'* Veranda Café. This was decorated with real palm trees and white wicker furniture, while ivy grew up the trellis-covered walls.

- 'You sank in it up to your knees,' said ship's baker Reginald Burgess of the carpet on the *Titanic*. Throughout the ship, great attention was paid to the design, with touches of Georgian, Louis XV and other historical styles blending with the latest fashions of the Edwardian era. In short, the *Titanic* was cool and classy.

- The designers wanted everyone on board to have a memorable experience, so though the third-class rooms were simple, they were still far more luxurious than most passengers would have been used to at home.

- Unlike modern ships, there were no shops on board, though two barbershops sold postcards and souvenirs such as White Star pennants and paperweights.

- As the ship was a byword for fashion, any manufacturer linked to the fitting-out of the

Titanic made the most of it: from Vinolia Otto toilet soap and Colman's mustard to the makers of the ship's doors, stationery and sofas.

- If passengers fell ill during the voyage, they could be brought to an ultramodern infirmary and operating room staffed by two doctors.

A titan of technology

The *Titanic* really was state of the art and sent the publicity department into overdrive:

- **Feel the power:** Electricity was generated by four 400-kilowatt engines and dynamos fitted in a separate, watertight engine room (so it would keep working in the unlikely event that the ship sprang a leak).

- **Bing!** The ship was lit by 10,000 electric lights, while the generators also powered some 150 electric motors, 75 fans, eight cargo cranes, winches, electric lifts, heaters, cookers, clocks and telegraphs. How thoroughly modern!

- **Did you call?** There were some 322 km of electric cables aboard, including 1,500 bell-pushes for summoning stewards.

- **This is your captain speaking:** The *Titanic* had a 50-phone switchboard with its own operator. These telephones were used by crew members in different parts of the ship, though none could be used to talk to anyone on land.

- **Wish you were here.** The Marconi wireless (radio) station magically allowed passengers and crew to send and receive telegrams over thousands of miles. Previously, the only way for a ship to contact others was through flags or signal lights.

- **A forest of instruments.** The bridge bristled with modern technology. The central wheelhouse held the main compass and a contraption known as the 'telemotor control wheel', which used hydraulics to steer the ship. In front of the wheelhouse were the docking and steering telegraphs, and telephones to other parts of the ship. In the chart room next door were the watertight door controller, the submarine signal receiver, the master clocks and other devices.

Bruce Ismay set a date of 20 March 1912 for the *Titanic*'s maiden voyage. In a flurry of activity, White Star began to issue timetables, posters and stationery advertising the March sailing. But a few weeks later – oops! – the *Olympic* collided with the Royal Navy cruiser HMS *Hawke*, leading some to fear that the superliners were just too big to handle. Though two of her watertight compartments were flooded, the *Olympic* made it safely back to port and there were no injuries, adding to the myth that she and her sister ship were unsinkable.

Work on the *Titanic* was delayed while repairs were hastily carried out on the *Olympic*. Though the date for the maiden voyage was put back to 10 April, Pirrie knew it was still going to take a frenzy of activity for the work to be completed on time, and he personally supervised the important stage of moving the *Titanic* into dry dock on 3 February 1912. Here the three gigantic propellers could be fitted and the hull painted.

☆

Those missing lifeboats

One of Harland & Wolff's directors, Alexander Carlisle, originally proposed using a new type of crane, or *davit*, which could handle more lifeboats than usual. This would enable the *Titanic* to carry up to 48 boats, more than enough to give everyone on board a seat.

But the *Titanic*'s designers decided that too many lifeboats would clutter the decks and detract from the feeling of space and luxury, so only 16 lifeboats were eventually fitted in January 1912, along with four collapsible boats (called Engelhardts, after their Danish inventor). Together these 20 lifeboats could hold 1,178 people – just over half the number on board.[9]

Amazingly, this was completely within the law. The British Board of Trade regulations were hopelessly out of date and didn't really cater for giant ships the size of the *Titanic*. Besides, no-one dreamed for a minute that the lifeboats would ever be needed. The *Titanic* was unsinkable, wasn't it?

9. The ship was also equipped with 3,560 lifejackets and 49 lifebuoys.

All the while, White Star churned out publicity to promote the maiden voyage. The whole point of building bigger and better ships was to make money, so the voyage needed to be a great success. White Star proclaimed their giant ships 'without peer on the ocean', and passengers were assured of 'comfort, elegance and security'.

Throughout March, workers burst their braces to the meet their deadlines. As the sea trials approached, the first crew members began to trickle on board, many of them engineers who would need time to get to know how the ship worked. By the end of March, the ship was finished and ready for her sea trials.

A safe pair of hands

'When anyone asks me how I can best describe my experience in nearly forty years at sea, I merely say, uneventful. Of course there have been winter gales, and storms and fog and the like. But in all my experience, I have never been in any accident...of any sort worth speaking about.'

Captain Edward J. Smith, speaking in 1907

Safe and seaworthy

On 2 April, ten months after her launch, the *Titanic* took to the open seas for the first time. On board were the proud designers Thomas Andrews and Edward Wilding, 78 members of the 'black gang' – stokers, greasers and firemen – and some 40 or so officers, crew and company officials. At the helm was Captain Edward J. Smith, who had more than 40 years' experience at sea. Nonetheless, he must have nervously eyed Mr Francis Carruthers, the Board of Trade surveyor, who was there to ensure that everything worked, and that the ship was fit to carry passengers.

At 6.00 a.m. the *Titanic* edged away from the jetty as four tugs towed her into open water. Crowds cheered and waved from the banks as the giant vessel slowly made her way down the narrow channel of Belfast Lough. Some 3 km off Carrickfergus, the tugs cast off their lines. A blue and white flag signalled: 'I am undergoing speed trials.' Steam rushed from the boilers to the two huge engines for the first time and, slowly but surely, *Titanic*'s propellers began to churn up the water.

Now for the science bit!

At full steam, the *Titanic*'s engines could produce the same power as an army of 59,000 horses (44 megawatts). For those of you who like your nuts and bolts, here's how it all worked:

- The *Olympic*-class liners were equipped with 29 triple-furnace boilers that created high-pressure steam. This drove the pistons in two sets of giant reciprocating engines nearly four storeys tall. Each set turned a three-blade propeller, one either side, measuring 7.2 m in diameter.

- The leftover steam from these engines was used to run a steam turbine. This turned the central four-blade propeller near the ship's rudder, which measured 5.2 m across.

- As 25 of the boilers were double-ended, there were 162 individual fires burning when all the ship's boilers were fired.

- Not surprisingly, all these engines belted out great clouds of smoke which were carried away by three giant funnels big enough to drive two trains through (the fourth funnel was a dummy, added for the sake of appearance). These towered 19 m above the deck, so that passengers could walk around on deck without being covered in soot.

In the open waters of the Irish Sea, the *Titanic* was put through her paces:

- **racing up to speeds of 20 knots (37 km/h)**
- **port and starboard turns at various speeds using rudder only and propellers only**
- **emergency stop with engines full astern (this took 800 metres)**
- **wheel hard over to turn full circle (diameter 3,520 m)**
- **four-hour cruise**
- **test lowering of the anchors.**

The *Titanic* passed all these tests with flying colours, and the trials took just one day. Why so short? The *Titanic*'s sister ship *Olympic* was already performing well, so everyone was pretty confident. The owners were also very keen to make sure the *Titanic* was all set for its sailing date of 10 April. They must have sighed with relief when Mr Carruthers duly signed the certificate of seaworthiness, and the *Titanic* was declared ready for her first voyage.

Shortly after 8.00 p.m. that night, the *Titanic* left Belfast, never to return. She was now bound for Southampton, a major port on the south coast of England. During a routine journey of 917 km, designer Thomas Andrews must have felt proud of his achievement. He jotted down a last-minute set of notes that would ensure the smooth running of the ship. Late the next evening, Wednesday 3 April, the *Titanic* docked safely in Berth 44 at Southampton. There were now just seven days until her maiden voyage to New York. So far, so good!

An unfortunate precedent

Sometimes described as the 'first *Titanic*', the White Star Line sailing ship RMS *Tayleur* ran aground and sank off Lambay Island in Dublin Bay during her maiden voyage on 21 January 1854. Out of the 652 people on board, 380 lives were lost, many of them emigrants travelling to Australia. Like the *Titanic*, the *Tayleur* was big, fast and technically advanced. However, her crew lacked experience and her magnetic compasses weren't adjusted to take account of the ship's iron hull.

There may be trouble ahead

- Morgan Robertson's short novel of 1898, *Futility, or the Wreck of the Titan*, features a gigantic luxury liner called the *Titan*, which is thought to be unsinkable. Sailing across the Atlantic in April, the liner hits an iceberg and sinks.[10] More than half the passengers are lost because there are not enough lifeboats on board. Other spooky similarities between the two ships are their size (800 ft long for *Titan*, 882½ ft for the *Titanic*) and speed (25 knots for *Titan*, 23 knots for *Titanic*).

- On 22 March 1886, journalist William Thomas Stead wrote a fictional article called 'How the Mail Steamer Went Down in Mid-Atlantic, by a Survivor'. He described how a steamer collided with another ship, with a great loss of life due to the lack of lifeboats. Stead added: 'This is exactly what might take place and will take place if liners are sent to sea short of boats.'

- Six years later, Stead published another story in which a White Star Line vessel, the *Majestic*, rescues survivors of another ship that collided with an iceberg, thanks to a premonition by a clairvoyant on board. Despite these predictions, Stead still boarded the *Titanic* at Southampton...

10. The shipping authorities knew of the dangers. Between January and July, vessels had to sail further south to avoid icebergs, adding 320 km to their route.

Mr Carter's motor car embarks for the journey of a lifetime

(see page 160)

Chapter Two

ALL ABOARD!

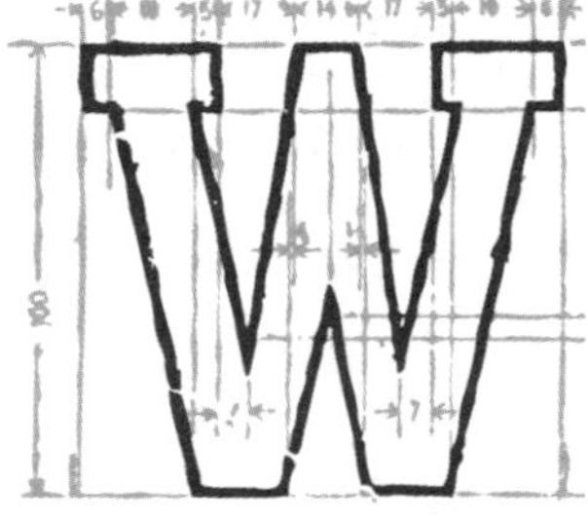

hen the *Titanic* arrived at the port of Southampton on 3 April 1912, there was still a mountain of work to be done. The next day, ship designer Thomas Andrews wrote to his wife: 'I think the ship will clean up all right before sailing' – but it would still take a frantic effort in the final few days to get everything ready in time.

☆

Unsolicited testimonials

Titanic's passengers certainly gave the new liner the thumbs up:

- 'The *Titanic* is a marvel I can tell you I have never seen such a sight in all my life, she is like a floating palace, everything up to date': Percy Andrew Bailey, 18, travelling alone to a new job as a butcher's apprentice in Ohio.
- 'The *Titanic* was wonderful, far more splendid and huge than I dreamed of. The other crafts in the harbour were like cockle shells beside her': Charlotte Collyer, heading to Idaho, USA to start a new life with her husband as a fruit farmer.
- 'What a ship...our rooms are furnished in the best of taste and most luxuriously': Ida Straus, American millionairess.
- 'The ship is like a palace. My cabin is ripping, hot and cold water and a very comfy looking bed and plenty of room': Lawrence Beesley, on his way to visit his brother in Toronto, Canada.
- 'We dined last night in the Ritz restaurant. It was the last word in luxury... the food was superb': First-class passenger Mrs Walter Douglas, heading home to Minnesota, USA.

Though White Star had been using Southampton since 1907, a new, larger dock had now been built specially for the *Titanic* and the *Olympic*. A 24-hour laundry was also built close to the quays, so that each time the ships docked, the dirty linen could quickly be unloaded and cleaned for the next voyage. Boat trains from London ran straight onto the quayside, so passengers had only a short walk to the ship.

Day after day, the fifteen quayside cranes and winches worked flat out as huge quantities of linen, bedding, cutlery, glassware, beer, foodstuffs and tableware were loaded aboard for the 1,300 passengers and 900-odd crew. Meanwhile a constant stream of trucks and carts brought almost 570 tonnes of cargo for shipping to the United States (amounting to 11,524 individual items). Putting freight on a passenger ship was the quickest way of moving it across the Atlantic. It was also a good money-spinner for White Star.[1]

1. There was also money to be made from carrying mail, and, as a British ship carrying letters and parcels, the Titanic *had the title RMS, or Royal Mail Steamer.*

Throughout the week, crowds of spectators gathered at the dock, dwarfed by the *Titanic*'s massive black steel exterior and smokestacks the height of a 25-storey building. On Good Friday, 5 April, the *Titanic* was 'dressed' from stem to stern in colourful signal flags and pennants in salute to the people of Southampton. Usually the public was allowed on board to tour the ship. Not this time – there was just too much left to be done.

Pride before a fall

'The White Star liners – eloquent testimonies to the progress of mankind, as shown in the conquest of mind over matter – will rank high in the achievements of the 20th century.'

White Star advertisement

Careful what you wish for

The passengers may have admired the facilities, but 34-year-old bedroom steward George Beedum was less impressed: 'My cold has been rotten...and what with no dusters or anything to work with I wish the bally ship at the bottom of the sea.'

Cargo and provisions

Brace yourself for a few more facts and figures. Prior to the voyage, the ship was stocked with tonne after tonne of provisions. The original manifest lists:

A vast supply of refrigerated food:

- Fresh meat: 75,000 lb (34,000 kg)
- Fresh fish: 11,000 lb (5,000 kg)
- Salt & dried fish: 4,000 lb (1,800 kg)
- Bacon and ham: 7,500 lb (3,400 kg)
- Poultry and game: 25,000 lb (11,340 kg)
- Fresh eggs: 40,000
- Sausages: 2,500 lb (1,130 kg)
- Potatoes: 40 tons (41 tonnes)
- Onions: 3,500 lb (1,600 kg)
- Tomatoes: 3,500 lb (1,600 kg)
- Fresh asparagus: 800 bundles
- Fresh green peas: 2,500 lb (1,130 kg)
- Lettuce: 7,000 heads
- Sweetbreads: 1,000
- Ice cream: 1,750 lb (800 kg)
- Coffee: 2,200 lb (1,000 kg)
- Tea: 800 lb (360 kg)
- Rice, dried beans etc.: 10,000 lb (4,540 kg)
- Sugar: 10,000 lb (4,540 kg)
- Flour: 250 barrels
- Cereals: 10,000 lb (4,540 kg)
- Apples: 36,000
- Oranges: 36,000
- Lemons: 16,000
- Grapes: 1,000 lb (454 kg)

- Grapefruit: 13,000
- Jams and marmalades: 1,120 lb (510 kg)
- Fresh milk: 1,500 gal (6,800 l)
- Fresh cream: 1,200 qt (1,360 l)
- Condensed milk: 600 gal (2,730 l)
- Fresh butter: 6,000 lb (2,720 kg)
- Ales and stout: 15,000 bottles
- Wines: 1,000 bottles
- Spirits: 850 bottles
- Minerals: 1,200 bottles
- Cigars: 8,000.

57,600 items of crockery and 29,000 pieces of glassware, including:

- Teacups: 3,000
- Dinner plates: 12,000
- Ice-cream plates: 5,500
- Soufflé dishes: 1,500
- Wine glasses: 2,000
- Salt shakers: 2,000
- Pudding dishes: 1,200
- Fingerbowls: 1,000.

44,000 pieces of cutlery, all specially designed for White Star, including:

- Oyster forks: 1,000
- Mustard spoons: 1,500
- Nutcrackers: 300
- Egg spoons: 2,000
- Grape scissors: 1,500
- Asparagus tongs: 400.

200,000 pieces of laundry, including:

- Aprons: 4,000
- Blankets: 7,500
- Bed sheets: 18,000
- Tablecloths: 6,000
- Bedcovers: 3,600
- Eiderdown quilts: 800
- Single sheets: 15,000
- Table napkins: 45,000
- Bath towels: 7,500
- Fine towels: 25,000
- Roller towels: 3,500
- Double sheets: 3,000
- Pillow slips: 15,000.

Also on board were 12 cases of ostrich plumes, 35 cases of books, 300 cases of walnuts, 117 cases of sponges, and a Renault car; not forgetting 50 cases of toothpaste, a cask of china headed for Tiffany's, five grand pianos, and 30 cases of golf clubs and tennis rackets. Brown Brothers and Co. shipped 76 cases of dragon's blood – sap from a Canary Islands palm tree, used to colour wood varnish and make-up.

Some wealthy passengers brought valuable works of art with them. Most spectacular was a jewelled copy of the *Rubaiyat*, a collection of poems attributed to the 11th-century Persian mathematician and astronomer Omar Khayyám. The cover was inlaid with 1,500 gems, each set in gold. It had just been sold at auction for £405 and was being delivered to its new owner, Gabriel Wells, a New York book dealer.

Embarkation

The next day – Saturday 6 April 1912 – 5,344 tonnes of coal were loaded into the ship's bunkers,[2] a thoroughly mucky business. It took 24 hours to coal a large liner like the *Titanic*, after which the ship's carpenter would seal up the coaling ports. Following that, every last deck, staircase and passageway had to be cleaned to remove the fine coating of black dust that settled on it during loading.

Getting enough coal had been a struggle. In early 1912, Britain was in the grip of the Great Coal Strike. Though this ended on 6 April, there wasn't enough time for newly mined coal to be shipped to Southampton and loaded onto the *Titanic*. White Star were determined to solve the problem by hook or by crook:

- **Supplies were brought over from the United States on the *Olympic*.**

- **Coal was removed from smaller liners, including White Star's *Oceanic* and *Majestic*.**

2. *The* Titanic *used 562–581 tonnes of coal a day when cruising at 21 knots (38.9 km/h).*

- **Several ships had their voyages cancelled, and some passengers were upgraded to the *Titanic* (would *you* have complained?).**

- **One story tells how George Frederick Bull, a bursar for the company, travelled with a colleague to Wallasey in Merseyside. There, it is said, they stole coal from the striking miners at gunpoint!**

Over the past few days, a skeleton crew had remained on board to keep the ship ticking over and provide steam, electricity and heat. But Saturday was recruitment day and the crew were signed on in their hundreds, many delighted to get back to work as the coal strike had led to mass unemployment.[3] Most were local men from Southampton, with the numbers made up by workers from Liverpool, London and Belfast.

3. Over 17,000 men were left without work in Southampton alone.

The crew

Deck crew (sailing the ship):

- **29 able seamen (ABs)** carried out the day-to-day operation of the ship. They were also trained to launch and man the lifeboats.

- **7 quartermasters** worked on and around the bridge. They helped to steer the ship, hoist signal flags and assist the Duty Officer with navigation.

- **6 lookouts** worked in pairs doing short two-hour shifts (because of the freezing temperatures) in the crow's nest (a perch halfway up the mainmast).

- **A lamp trimmer** tended to the few old-fashioned oil lamps on board, such as the signal lamps that indicated port and starboard. His job was to trim the wicks so they burned cleanly and evenly, which made them last longer.

- **The master-at-arms** and his assistant took charge of the gun cabinet (the only other person who had the keys was the Chief Officer).

Engineering crew (doing the dirty work down below in the engine and boiler rooms; known as the 'black gang'):

- **25 engineers and 20 electricians** kept the engines, generators and other equipment running smoothly. It was a skilled job, so they were the highest-paid of the crew.

- **33 greasers** worked alongside the engineers – they made sure the engines and other machinery were properly oiled and lubricated.

- **176 firemen or stokers** did the back-breaking work of shovelling coal in the furnaces. As temperatures in the boiler rooms could reach 50°C, they wore just their vests and shorts. They worked around the clock in shifts of 4 hours on and 8 hours off.

- **73 coal trimmers** had one of the dirtiest (and worst-paid) jobs on board, shovelling the coal down to the firemen below. They also had to keep the great mounds of coal level, since if it built up too much on one side the ship might list (lean sideways) or even capsize.

Victualling crew (looking after the passengers):

- **62 chefs, bakers and butchers** prepared and cooked the meals. These included a kosher cook who prepared food for Jewish passengers, and 36 glassmen, plate-washers and scullerymen who did the washing up.

- **322 stewards** doing a wide range of jobs:

  - **Bedroom stewards** made the beds, cleaned cabins and delivered meals.

  - **Linen stewards** maintained all the linen on board (bed sheets, bathroom towels, tablecloths, etc.).

  - **'Glory-hole' stewards** had the job of cleaning toilets throughout the ship.

  - **Bellboys**, nicknamed 'Buttons', carried luggage, ran errands, delivered telegrams and operated lifts. Some were just 14 or 15 years old.

  - **12 stewards** served food to the rest of the crew.

  - **9 men** shined the shoes of first-class passengers.

There were 23 female crew members: 18 stewardesses, two cashiers, a masseuse, a Turkish Bath attendant, and a matron who acted as chaperone for single women in third class (to stop them being pestered by men).

Other crew members included the purser's four clerks, bartenders, barbers, two carpenters, a night watchman, florists, two window cleaners, swimming-bath attendants, a gym instructor and a squash coach.

Wait – there's more!

- **43 personal valets, chauffeurs, nurses and maids** were also brought on the trip by wealthy passengers used to extra pampering. Personal servants were given cabins close to their employers, while chauffeurs and chefs were put in second-class accommodation.
- **Eight bandsmen** led by violinist Wallace Henry Hartley. The musicians were divided into two groups: a five-piece band that played for first-class passengers at teatime, after-dinner concerts and Sunday services, and a trio that played in the second-class à la carte restaurant and Verandah café. Not officially part of the crew, they travelled as second-class passengers.
- **Guarantee group.** This team of nine highly skilled Harland & Wolff engineers was led by Thomas Andrews. They accompanied the *Titanic* to see to unfinished work and tend to any teething problems that might crop up on the maiden voyage to New York.
- **Two operators** worked in the wireless room.
- **Five postal clerks** worked in the mail room.

The officers

- **Captain Edward John Smith** began working for the White Star Line in 1887, and during his career captained 17 ships for the company. Considered White Star's best captain, he commanded new ships for their sea trials and was the natural choice to skipper the *Titanic* as he had already captained the *Olympic* for several months. A cheery chap, he was well liked by wealthy passengers and was known as 'the millionaire's captain'. Smith earned £105 a month (300 times as much as a stewardess), plus a bonus of £200 if no ship in his command had an accident.

- **Chief Officer Henry Tingle Wilde.** There had been a reshuffle of officers at Southampton, bringing in Wilde as another officer with sufficient experience to handle a big ship like the *Titanic*. As a result, Murdoch and Lightoller were bumped down at short notice, which probably ruffled a few feathers (not ideal in an emergency).

- **First Officer William McMaster Murdoch.** Born into a family of seafarers, he joined the White Star Line in 1899. Four years later his quick thinking stopped the White Star liner *Arabic* from colliding with another ship in the darkness. Like Smith and Wilde, he was aboard the *Olympic* when it hit HMS *Hawke* in September 1911 (see page 40).

- **Second Officer Charles Herbert Lightoller** was regarded as something of a 'hard case'. At the age of 16 Lightoller had been shipwrecked on a deserted island, then a few years later almost died from malaria. In 1898 he abandoned the sea and spent a year prospecting for gold in Canada's frozen northwest, but he arrived home penniless a year later. He joined White Star in 1900 and slowly worked his way up the ranks, becoming first mate on the *Oceanic*.

- **Third Officer Herbert John 'Bert' Pitman** was responsible for taking readings from the sun and stars, supervising the decks, and relieving bridge officers when required.

- **Fourth Officer Joseph Boxhall** was in charge of updating the ship's charts and scheduling watches.

- **Fifth Officer Harold Lowe.** Despite many years at sea, the maiden voyage of the *Titanic* was to be his first transatlantic crossing.

- **Sixth Officer James Paul Moody** was responsible for measuring air and water temperatures – and for closing the last gangway onto the ship.

- **Purser Herbert McElroy** was in charge of accounts, ticketing, luggage requests and the ship's safe.

The next day was Easter Sunday, so all work aboard the *Titanic* ceased for the day. It was the calm before the storm. Time was running out and the next day the docks were chock-a-block as supplies of fresh food were loaded into the large refrigerators and storerooms on G Deck. No-one was busier than Thomas Andrews, who all week showed parties of VIPs around the ship and sorted out countless details with officials, agents and staff.[4] On Tuesday 9 April, the day before the voyage, the endless cascade of cargo and provisions continued. But as darkness came, the quays fell quiet again.

Sailing day!

Just after dawn on Wednesday 10 April 1912, the bulk of the crew began to stream onto the giant liner from all over Southampton. First on board, at 6.00 a.m., were Thomas Andrews and his crack engineering team from Harland & Wolff. Already the ship was buzzing with activity. Some of the crew gathered at the

4. The obsessive Andrews couldn't help himself: his personal secretary noted how he fiddled with the placing of individual tables, chairs and fans until they were just so.

lifeboats to perform a drill for the Board of Trade's Captain Clarke, who was aboard to give the *Titanic* the final all-clear.[5] Eighteen crew members were lowered in two lifeboats and rowed around briefly to ensure that the boats were in good working order – no problems there.

Later, at 9.30 a.m., White Star managing director J. Bruce Ismay, along with his wife and family, gave the ship a final tour of inspection. Around this time, the early train arrived from London's Waterloo railway station,[6] bringing more than 200 second-class passengers and nearly 500 third-class. They came from all walks of life: painters, teachers, farmers, labourers and miners. Some travelled in families, others alone. When the train arrived at Southampton docks, they were transferred straight onto the ship, along with passengers from other White Star liners whose voyages had been cancelled due to the coal strike.

5. Captain Clarke also checked that systems such as fresh water supply, food stowage and passenger accommodation were up to scratch, and ensured that the Titanic *had enough coal aboard. He signed the Report of Survey of an Immigrant Ship, allowing the* Titanic *to set sail.*
6. a journey of 130 km.

Crowds of people swarmed along the pier while porters manhandled luggage aboard. It would have been hard not to stop and gawp at the gleaming black hull of the *Titanic* as it towered over the quays. For the next two hours, second-class passengers and reporters were free to tour the delights of first class. Many were bowled over by the elegance of the first-class public rooms, the amazing exercise machines in the gymnasium and the sheer size of the vessel.

The arrival of the special boat train around 11.30 a.m. brought over 170 first-class passengers. Fashionably late, they boarded just 30 minutes before sailing time. Each class had its own separate gangways to go on board. First-class passengers were given a warm welcome by Chief Steward Latimer and his team in the main reception rooms – male passengers were even given a flower to put in their buttonhole. Then they were escorted to their staterooms (cabins).

Third-class passengers received a rather different welcome: a check by a medical officer to ensure they were healthy enough to pass US customs. Their tickets were stamped with a berth number, then they were left to find their own bunk. Though stewards no doubt tried to direct the crowd, Eastern European and Scandinavian passengers with little English must have found it very hard to navigate through the labyrinth of halls and stairways.

Once the *Titanic* was underway, passengers in the three different classes would live completely separate lives, so that the posh folks wouldn't have to rub shoulders with the common mob from steerage. Heaven forbid! They ate in separate dining rooms, read and talked in separate lounges, smoked in separate smoking rooms and used different gangways to move around the ship.[7]

As midday approached, the *Titanic*'s decks became crowded with passengers lining the rails, waiting to watch as they left port. The greatest passenger ship ever built was now ready to begin her maiden voyage!

7. A long, wide passage along E Deck used by those in steerage class was nicknamed Scotland Road after a busy working-class street in Liverpool, while a corridor for first-class use was called Park Lane after the fashionable street in London.

The passengers

There were 1,317 passengers on board when the *Titanic* headed out across the Atlantic:[8]

- **324 first-class passengers** (average ticket £86 or $430, while a deluxe parlour suite cost a wallet-whacking £660 ($3,300))
- **284 second-class passengers** (average ticket £13 or $65), including businessmen, members of the clergy, a teacher, a chauffeur and eight musicians
- **709 in third class, or 'steerage'** (average ticket £7 or $35), mostly European emigrants.
- These totals include 103 children – five in first class, 22 in second and 76 in third class.
- The biggest family on board was the Sage family from Peterborough: John and Annie brought all nine children with them, aged between 4 and 20.

8. This figure is only one estimate. There was no precise record of everyone on board, as lists were handwritten and were copied by different people. Last-minute bookings and cancellations, plus people who missed the ship, make it impossible to say exactly how many people were on board. Other passengers traded or sold their boarding passes, and the names of the replacement passengers were never recorded.

- The youngest passenger was 2-month-old Millvina Dean, travelling in third class with her parents and 1-year-old brother Bertram.

- 13 couples were travelling on honeymoon.

- 15 passengers were probably travelling under false names. Michel Navratil used the name 'Mr Hoffman' to escape his wife, whom he left in France. He had taken his two young sons with him. Alfred Nourney cheekily called himself 'Baron von Drachstedt' to blag a first-class room even though he only paid for second class. Three professional gamblers also travelled under false names: Charles H. Romaine, George 'Boy' Brereton and Harry 'Kid' Homer. White Star had been alerted and posted a message warning passengers that cardsharps were on board.

- At least 30 different nationalities travelled on the *Titanic*. Most passengers were from England, Ireland or the United States. There were also quite a few from Sweden, Finland, Norway, Canada and Syria. Other passengers came from as far afield as Argentina, Thailand, India, China, Bulgaria, Peru, Turkey, Japan and Mexico.

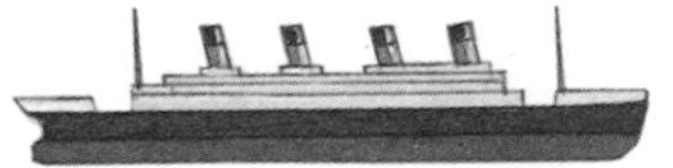

A ruff crossing?

- There were at least nine dogs on board the *Titanic* – a real luxury, as their owners had to pay half-fare for them, the same as for a child – a Newfoundland, two Pomeranians, a chow chow, a Pekinese called Sun Yat-sen (the name of China's new president in 1912), an Airedale terrier named Kitty, two French bulldogs, including a champion named Gamon de Pycombe, and a small dog named Frou Frou.

- Five lucky dogs stayed with their owners in their cabins (the others were locked in kennels), and every day a crew member took all the dogs for walks around the after decks. Passenger and artist Francis Millet sniffily wrote to a friend from Queenstown that the ladies in first class 'carried tiny dogs and led husbands around like pet lambs'. An unofficial dog show was even planned in first class for Monday 15 April, to be held on the grand staircase.

- Also on board were four hens and cockerels owned by Marie G. Young (who had once taught the piano to US president Theodore Roosevelt's daughter). During the voyage two second-class passengers, Nellie Hocking and Edwina Trout, were woken by the sound of a cock crowing, and took it as a sign of bad luck!

- The *Titanic* had its own pet cat called Jenny – the ship's rat-catcher. While in Southampton, Jenny had kittens and, according to some crew members, left the ship.

- A free ride? Though the *Titanic* was spanking new, it's more than likely that a few Belfast rats snuck on board, lured by the warmth and the smell of all those tasty provisions. A number of rats were seen 'fleeing' the forward boiler rooms the day before the collision, and another ran across the floor during a party in steerage on the night of 14 April. No doubt the hulking ship was also home to its fair share of cockroaches, dust mites and the usual bugs.

- Perhaps you've heard the various myths about curious creatures on board, including an elephant, a pack of hunting hounds and a pig. None are true. Edith Rosenbaum[9] did take on board a 'lucky' musical pig, but this was a stuffed toy.

9. later known as Edith Russell – she changed her name after the First World War so as not to be thought German.

Stoking *Titanic*'s boilers

Titanic's technology still relied on muscle power

Chapter Three

THE MAIDEN VOYAGE

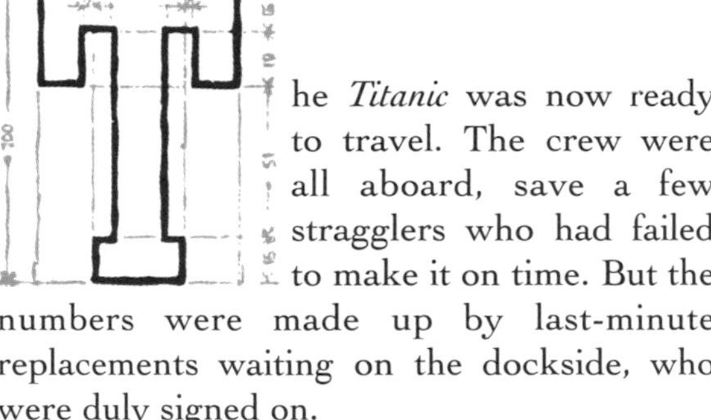

The *Titanic* was now ready to travel. The crew were all aboard, save a few stragglers who had failed to make it on time. But the numbers were made up by last-minute replacements waiting on the dockside, who were duly signed on.

Just-missed-it club

Despite White Star's best efforts to make everything run to schedule, some passengers were reluctant to book a ticket while the coal strike was on. As a result, the ship wasn't fully booked up for her maiden voyage. Other passengers and crew just didn't make it on board before the ship sailed.

- A total of 22 recruits failed to board in time. Steward P. Kilford left because he was sick. Ship's fireman Thomas Hart got drunk after signing on for the voyage, and his discharge book (official record of service) was stolen and used by someone else to get aboard. Hart was too embarrassed to return home until weeks after the sinking (8 May), though his mother was very happy to see him as she was busy arranging a memorial service for him. The three Slade brothers, scheduled to work as stokers on the *Titanic*, were out drinking to celebrate a birthday. Leaving the pub a little too late, they just missed the gangplank and the ship sailed without them.

- Another name not appearing on the crew list was David (Davy) Blair, who joined *Titanic* at Belfast as Second Officer, but was reassigned to the *Oceanic* at Southampton. Blair wrote in a postcard to his sister: 'This is a magnificent ship, I feel very disappointed I am not to make her first voyage.'

Some 55 passengers cancelled their bookings for all sorts of reasons:

- **Too busy:** J. Pierpont Morgan, the US millionaire who had funded the building of the *Titanic*, was forced to cancel his journey due to business meetings.

- **In a hurry:** Mr and Mrs J. Horace Harding took Morgan's suite of rooms, but cancelled their booking to get an earlier sailing date aboard the *Mauretania*.

- **Injured:** US steel magnate Henry Frick booked a suite in February 1912 but cancelled after his wife sprained her ankle during a Mediterranean cruise.

- **Warned off:** Mr George W. Vanderbilt and his wife Edith changed their minds after a family member told them not to travel on a maiden voyage as 'so many things can go wrong'. They cancelled just three days before sailing. As their luggage had already been placed aboard, one of their servants stayed with it.

- **Spooked:** Mrs Edward W. Bill refused to board after having a nightmare of the *Titanic* sinking.

The *Milwaukee Journal* reported that the number of people who claimed they had just missed the boat – around 6,000 – could have filled two or three *Titanics*!

A voyage to remember

Like the launch, the maiden voyage was a major occasion. The *Titanic* was *the* ship to travel on. For first-class passengers this was an important social event, and they would be able to brag about their trip on the world's most luxurious and modern ship. It was safe, too – a comforting thought for passengers in all classes, including those in steerage who would be making a one-way journey. Many of them, looking forward to a better life in America, were carrying all they owned in a couple of bags or a trunk.

Just before noon on 10 April 1912, the Blue Peter[1] was hoisted up *Titanic*'s foremast, then three mighty blasts on the ship's whistles told everyone for miles around that the giant liner was about to set sail. On the docks the crowds waved goodbye, mingling their shouted farewells with the jolly ragtime tunes played by the ship's orchestra high up on the boat deck.

1. a signal flag indicating that a ship is about to depart.

In a great cloud of smoke and steam, the gangway was withdrawn, the mooring lines were cast off and the ship eased from her berth. Five tiny tugboats went to work, pulling the monster liner out into the River Test. At first, the crowds followed the ship along the dock. Once the tugs had manoeuvred the steamship through a 90-degree turn so she pointed downstream, they dropped their lines. The *Titanic*'s thunderous engines throbbed into life and the liner began to move under her own steam.

As the *Titanic* headed down Southampton Water,[2] Captain Smith's chest must have swelled with pride. He planned to retire after this voyage, and commanding the most famous ship in the world would be a fitting end to a very successful career. But the *Titanic*'s colossal size meant that she was especially hard to handle in the narrow channel of the River Test. Just a few minutes into the voyage, she approached a much smaller liner, the *New York*, moored alongside a pier.

2. the estuary of the rivers Test and Itchen.

On the *New York*'s deck a crowd had gathered to watch the *Titanic* pass. Their cheers turned into shrieks of horror as the turbulence of the *Titanic*'s engines and the sucking effect created by her giant hull caused the *New York* to snap her mooring lines with an almighty bang.[3] The crowd parted like the Red Sea as groups of spectators tried to escape the flying cable ends, and the gangway went crashing into the water. Worse still, the stern of the *New York* swung out into the river towards the bows of the oncoming *Titanic*.

Captain Smith quickly ordered 'full astern' and the lumbering giant reversed her engines in the nick of time[4] – the two ships came within 1.5 m of each other, the width of your outstretched arms. Captain Smith must have heaved a huge sigh of relief (he'd crunched the *Olympic* just seven months before; see page 40). It was another hour before the *New York* was safely shunted out of harm's way.

3. *They were made of twisted steel and 75 mm thick.*
4. *Other witnesses gave credit to the tug* Vulcan *for nudging the* New York *out of the way.*

Not a great start to the journey of a lifetime! While some on board muttered that this was a bad sign so early in the voyage, others put it out of their minds and made the most of their splendid surroundings. But the near-miss was not the only worry: a fire that had broken out in coal room No. 5 several days earlier in Southampton was still burning. A team of eight to ten stokers on each watch had orders to keep the fire hosed down, but it took three days to eventually put it out.

Without any further drama, the *Titanic* headed out into the open sea beyond, with the Isle of Wight on the starboard side. She steamed towards Cherbourg on the coast of Normandy, France, a journey of some 110 km. Any nerves the passengers may have had must have been settled during this peaceful crossing of the English Channel, which took five hours. Nonetheless, the delay caused by the *New York* incident meant that the ship arrived after sunset. In the darkness a further 274 passengers boarded, while others left the ship, including a yellow canary belonging to a Mr Meanwell.[5] Many of the most famous passengers met the ship here, including American millionaire John Jacob Astor (on honeymoon with his new wife, Madeleine), Benjamin Guggenheim, Margaret Tobin Brown, Charlotte Cardeza and Sir Cosmo and Lady Duff Gordon.

5. It had cost him 25¢ to ferry the bird across the Channel – surely the cheapest fare on board!

The rich and famous

Titanic's reputation for luxury attracted many wealthy industrialists and their families, who were willing to pay big bucks for the best suites and staterooms:[6]

- **Benjamin Guggenheim**, the naughty millionaire playboy, was travelling on the *Titanic* with his latest mistress, the French singer Léontine Aubart. Though he inherited a vast fortune from money made in mining and smelting, he had squandered most of it by the time he died.
- **Colonel John Jacob Astor IV**, one of the world's richest men at the time, was thought to be worth $150 million. Grandson of a wealthy fur trader, he had built up an impressive real-estate empire including many hotels. Astor also had a reputation as a playboy, and after a scandalous divorce had slunk off to Europe and Egypt with his new 19-year-old wife to escape attention.
- **Sir Cosmo and Lady Duff Gordon** travelled under the name Morgan; perhaps they wanted to avoid attention, or maybe they hoped to confuse the US Customs due to unpaid debts in America. Sir Cosmo was a wealthy Scottish landowner who had also won a silver medal for fencing in the 1906 Summer Olympics.

6. The combined wealth of the richest first-class passengers was estimated at $600 million (equivalent to $10 billion today).

His wife Lucy was a famous dress designer whose clients included the British royal family and theatre stars.

- **Isidor Straus**, worth some $50 million, co-owned the famous Macy's department store in New York (which still operates today) and had also been a Congressman for New York. He and his wife Ida (see page 1) were on their way home after a holiday on the French Riviera.

- **Margaret Tobin Brown** was the wife of a Colorado silver-mine magnate. For her role in the events that followed, she became known as 'the Unsinkable Molly Brown'.

- **Charlotte Martinez-Cardeza** was a rich US socialite. Her fortune came from her father, a British industrialist who was one of the first to manufacture denim jeans. After divorcing her husband, a Spanish nobleman, in 1900, she spent her time going on big-game safaris. Returning from one such safari, Mrs Cardeza took the largest suite of rooms on the *Titanic* and brought the most luggage: 14 steamer trunks containing 70 dresses, 10 fur coats and 91 pairs of gloves.

- **Harry Molson** was a member of the famous beer-brewing family and president of Molson's Bank in Montreal, Canada. Molson was a keen sailor who had already been in two shipping accidents. In 1899 he swam away from the *Scotsman* as it sank in the Gulf of St

Lawrence, and in 1904 he jumped through the window of his cabin and swam to shore after the *Canada* collided with another ship in the St Lawrence River.

- **Major Archibald Butt** was a military advisor to US president William Howard Taft.
- **John B. Thayer** was vice-president of the Pennsylvania Railroad and a first-class cricketer.
- US millionaire **George D. Widener** inherited his father's streetcar (tram) business. He was in France with his wife Eleanor to find a French chef for their new hotel in Philadelphia, the Ritz Carlton.
- **Walter D. Douglas** was the heir to the Quaker Oats fortune, worth millions.
- **Dorothy Gibson**, a 28-year-old silent film star, model and singer, was one of the highest-paid actresses in the world when she retired in May 1912.
- **Jacques Futrelle**, a famous journalist and mystery writer, is best known for his tales of Professor Augustus S. F. X. Van Dusen, known as 'the Thinking Machine' for using logic to crack a tricky case.

The *Titanic* was far too big for Cherbourg's little port, so passengers and luggage were brought to the ship by White Star's tenders, the small steamships *Nomadic* and *Traffic*.[7] A big door opened in the ship's side, and a gangway was put out for travellers to get on board. After being taken to their berths, they were shown where to get lifebelts and other life-saving gear, just in case. Around 90 minutes later the crew hauled up the giant anchor, and at 8.10 p.m. the *Titanic* headed for Queenstown (now Cobh) on the southern Irish coast.

After enjoying dinner, the passengers trickled back to their suites and rooms for their first night at sea. But there was no rest for the 'black gang' stoking the boilers below decks, or for Thomas Andrews's guarantee group helping to fine-tune the running of the ship. Every ship was unique, so it was a learning process even for experienced crew members.

7. *In February 2011 Harland & Wolff was awarded a contract to restore the* Nomadic *in time for the 2012* Titanic *centenary. The only White Star Line vessel still afloat, she has ferried many famous names out to ocean liners, including Charlie Chaplin, Elizabeth Taylor and Richard Burton.*

Death appears!

The *Titanic*'s fourth funnel, the one furthest aft (at the back), was a dummy. Captain Smith was furious when a stoker climbed to the top of the funnel at Queenstown and peered out to admire the view, thereby proving it was fake. Later, the sight of the smiling, black-faced worker led to rumours that Death himself had made an appearance. But why was the false funnel built in the first place?

- The ship's designers thought four funnels made the ship look more impressive.

- More funnels sold more tickets, as there was a belief among emigrants (many of whom didn't read but looked at the pictures of the ships they were sailing on) that the more funnels a ship had, the faster it was. The funnels were raked back at an angle to enhance the 'go-faster' look.

- The rival Cunard Line's ships *Mauretania* and *Lusitania* had four funnels, so White Star did not want to be outdone.

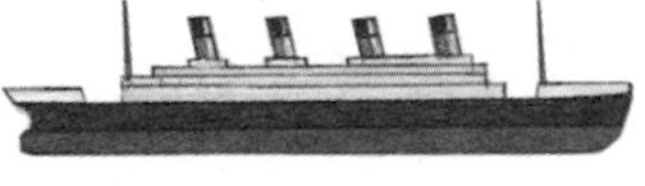

An emergency drill was carried out down below. Alarm bells rang out and the watertight doors slowly closed, sealing off the different compartments in the hull. This was standard procedure, and one visitor commented: 'None of us had the slightest fear…she was the last word in modern efficiency and was said to be literally unsinkable.' The next morning the passengers tucked into their first breakfast at sea, and by 11.00 a.m. the *Titanic* had anchored off Roche's Point, 3 km from Queenstown. She was met by a fleet of small vessels, or 'bumboats', which carried sellers of Irish lace, linen, china and other souvenirs. The traders set up a small market on the aft promenade deck and did a roaring trade.[8]

Two small tenders with paddlewheels, *America* and *Ireland*, ferried passengers, luggage and mailbags to and from the superliner. Seven passengers left the ship at Queenstown – and a 28-year-old fireman, John Coffey, deserted ship by smuggling himself ashore under some mail sacks. He had probably signed on to get a free ride home to Ireland.

8. John Jacob Astor is said to have bought a lace shawl for his wife Madeleine costing the huge sum of £165 ($825).

Caught on camera

One passenger who left at Queenstown was 32-year-old teacher Francis M. Browne, who later became a priest. Just a few days before, he had received a surprise in the post: a first-class ticket from Southampton to Queenstown, paid for by his uncle, the bishop of Cloyne.

Frank Browne was a keen photographer and took some great shots on the voyage, including pictures of Captain Smith, the Marconi room, and the anchor being raised for the last time. These photographs later appeared on the front pages of newspapers around the world.

An American millionaire even offered to pay Frank's way for the rest of the voyage to New York. But when his superior heard about this he cabled Queenstown saying: 'GET OFF THAT SHIP – PROVINCIAL.'

Frank accompanied the family of Lily Odell. She also took pictures, including the last ever photograph of the *Titanic* leaving Queenstown, taken from a tender.

For 25 years after Frank Browne's death, over 40,000 negatives lay forgotten in a metal trunk. When they were rediscovered by chance in 1986, an editor at the *Sunday Times* newspaper in London described them as 'the photographic equivalent to the discovery of the Dead Sea Scrolls'.

Thursday 11 April was a beautiful spring day. At 1.30 p.m. the starboard anchor was raised for the last time, and 25 minutes later *Titanic* was on her way once more. On the third-class promenade deck, Eugene Daly said farewell to Ireland by playing 'Erin's Lament' on his uilleann pipes.[9] Like many others, Daly was emigrating to the United States and never expected to return to his home country.

The ocean was as flat as a pancake – passenger Colonel Archibald Gracie called it a 'sea of glass' – and soon the *Titanic* was gliding along the south coast of Ireland. For the next three days the great ship sped steadily westwards across the Atlantic. The weather remained chilly but fine, and the calm waters made for the smoothest of journeys. The passengers had plenty of time to explore the ship and make the most of the opulent surroundings, fine food and entertainment on board. And all the while, *Titanic*'s vast crew worked hard to ensure that passengers enjoyed the trip of a lifetime.

9. Erin is the Irish name for Ireland. The uilleann pipes are traditional Irish bagpipes; uilleann *means 'elbow' in Irish, as the elbows are used to work the bellows and bag that pump air into the pipes.*

fun for all

First-class passengers could enjoy:

- The Turkish baths (at $1 a ticket), a suite of rooms including a steam room, a hot room, a warm room and a cooling room. One hi-tech piece of equipment was like a bed with a set of electric bulbs under the cover; their heat was thought to be good for the health.

- A bracing swim (25¢ a ticket) in one of the world's first onboard pools, which was filled with sea water.

- A game of squash (50¢) in the court on G Deck, or a lesson with the ship's resident professional, Fred Wright.

- A range of exercise machines in the gymnasium. As well as the usual selection of Indian clubs, rowing machines and bike machines, there were two electric horses for those accustomed to a morning gallop – a White Star advert showed passengers wearing full riding dress! Then it was on to the 'camel', a machine for strengthening the back and stomach muscles, before being pummelled by the mechanical hammers of the massage machine. Children were allowed to use the machines between 1.00 and 3.00 p.m. each day. Gym instructor T. W. McCawley showed passengers how to use all this equipment safely.

- Lots of organised entertainment, such as parties, balls, dances and games. As well as the five-piece orchestra, there was an electric organ on A Deck.

- Strolling on deck, or playing deck games such as quoits or something called 'bull ball'.

- Sending messages to friends and relatives via the wireless room.

- A game of billiards or cards. Betting was not encouraged, apart from the 'ship's pool', in which passengers placed bets on the number of miles that the *Titanic* was going to travel in the next 24 hours. The winner got all the money collected, minus 10 per cent for seamen's charities.

- Relaxing in deckchairs; chairs and blankets could be rented for the week at a cost of $1 each.

- Taking photos and developing them in the fully equipped darkroom on A Deck.

- Reading in the first-class library.

- Looking fabulous. Thanks to the strict Edwardian dress codes, wealthy women changed their clothes up to five times a day. What one wore to breakfast, lunch or tea, or to promenade on deck, was simply not acceptable at dinner! The evening was a time to show off the very latest fashions from Paris as one paraded down the grand staircase before dinner, or appeared magically in one of the ship's three first-class lifts.

Second-class options were more limited:

- There was a piano for sing-songs, and tables for cards or for games such as chess and dominoes.
- You could enjoy a stroll or sit in a deckchair on the various decks reserved for second-class passengers.
- You could read, chat or smoke in the second-class library or smoking room. A daily newspaper, the *Atlantic Daily Bulletin*, was printed aboard ship. As well as news articles, horse-racing results and society gossip, it contained the day's menu.
- Children of all classes brought their own toys, such as the spinning top owned by 6-year-old Douglas Spedden. They also played group games such as 'horse racing' on deck.

Dining with the captain was a traditional onboard treat.

Third-class passengers were very much left to make their own fun:

- They met friends in the third-class lounge, known as the 'general room', or played cards and smoked in the smoke room.
- They walked or sat on benches on the third-class deck.
- Edward Ryan, who joined at Queenstown, later wrote how easy it was to make friends on board. There were several musicians travelling in third class, and Ryan enjoyed dancing, singing and playing games. On the night of Sunday 14 April there was a concert in the dining room attended by around 300 people, with passengers taking turns to do their party pieces.
- With only two bathtubs for more than 700 passengers in third class, it would have been hard to have a relaxing soak. In fact, most passengers shared bathrooms, apart from a privileged few in the big suites.

But...

Mealtimes were probably the most popular events on board (at least for those who didn't get seasick), as many of the passengers ate far better aboard the *Titanic* than they ever had at home.

The routine of days at sea centred around meals. First-class passengers expected the very best – tables were set with elegant china, shining silverware and sparkling cut crystal, while the waiting staff saw to their every need. First-class passengers were called to lunch and dinner by the sound of ship's bugler P. W. Fletcher playing the patriotic tune 'The Roast Beef of Old England' (see page 180). Guests could also snack at the Verandah Café, which served coffee and elegant little sandwiches. However, though first-class passengers could ask for morning tea to be brought to their cabins, breakfast would have to wait until they shuffled down to the dining saloon.

Despite a nerve-wracking start to the voyage, all in all Captain Smith must have been pleased with the progress so far. By noon on Sunday 14 April the *Titanic* had travelled some 2,300 km, and there was a good chance that she would arrive ahead of schedule, early in the morning of Wednesday 17 April.[10] It was all such a marvellous adventure…

10. The ship was following a typical course for steamers at this time of year, known as the Outward Southern Track. This followed a great circle from the Fastnet Light off the southwest coast of Ireland to the Nantucket Shoal lightship off the coast of the United States.

Bad vibes

Despite the relatively smooth crossing, not everyone was able to relax:

- Chief Officer Henry Wilde sent a worried letter from Queenstown to his sister saying: 'I still don't like this ship, I have a queer feeling about it.'

- English journalist William Thomas Stead (see page 47) was warned by a fortune-teller not to travel across the ocean, but couldn't turn down an invite from US president William Howard Taft to speak at a peace conference. Poor Stead was also plagued by nightmares of shipwrecks.

- According to her daughter Eva (7 years old at the time), passenger Evelyn Hart didn't get a wink of sleep as she was afraid there might be an accident.

- Another passenger, Alfred Rowe, wrote to his wife Constance that he thought the ship was 'too big' and a 'positive danger'. His letter was posted from Queenstown and first came to light in 2007, 95 years after the disaster.

Evil omens

Given that there were over 2,000 people on board, it was inevitable that some of them would feel nervous before the crossing. And don't forget, sailors are a superstitious bunch:

- Flat-footed people and redheads bring bad luck to a ship.
- Disaster will follow if you step into a boat with your left foot first.
- Salt must be thrown over the left shoulder to keep evil spirits away.
- Cutting your hair or nails on board will bring bad luck.
- The expression 'touch wood' (or 'knock on wood' in American English) may come from knocking on a ship's hull to see if it was sturdy and free from rot.
- Looking back after a ship has left port also brings bad luck.

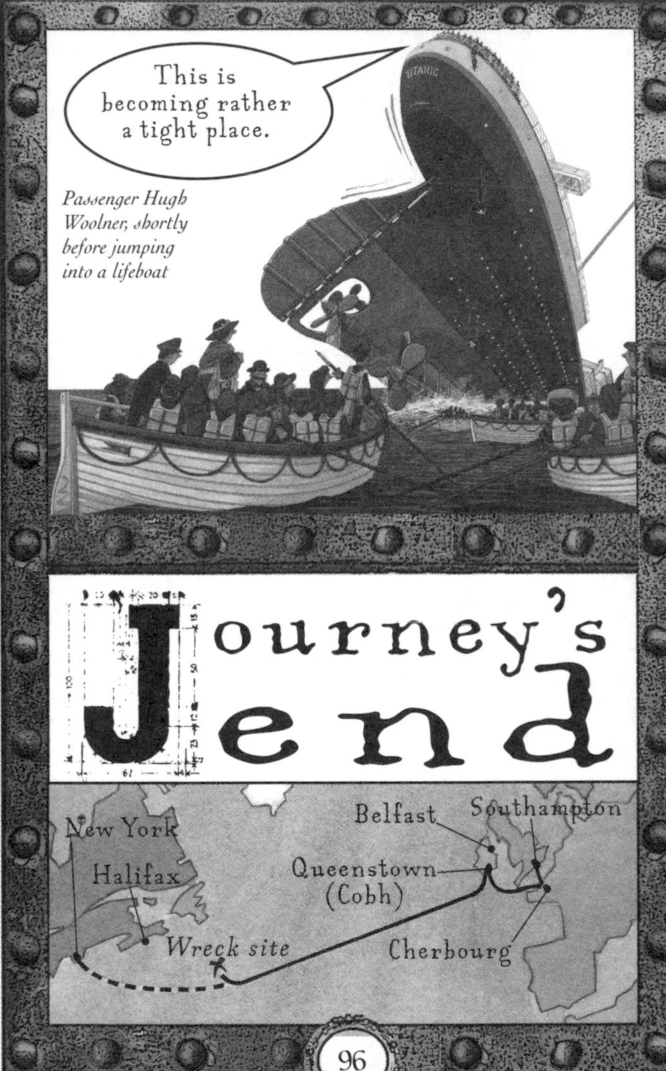

Passenger Hugh Woolner, shortly before jumping into a lifeboat

Chapter four

ICEBERG, DEAD AHEAD!

By Sunday 14 April, the *Titanic* was about 650 km from Newfoundland in Canada. For several days, radio messages from other ships had warned of icebergs ahead.[1] Captain Smith, like most commanders at the time, ordered his officers to steer 16 km further south but to maintain speed. Two extra boilers had been lit earlier that day, and the ship was travelling at 22 knots, close to full speed.

1. The winter of 1911–1912 was unusually mild in the Arctic. As a result, more icebergs broke away from the Greenland ice shelf and drifted further south – in contrast to the Antarctic, where explorer Captain Robert Scott's team died during the bitterest winter for years.

You have been warned!

As early as Friday 12 April, several ships, including the French liner *La Touraine*, had reported ice. There were three ice warnings on the Saturday, including one sent by a signal lamp from the passing steamer *Rappahannock*, and six more the following day:

- **At 9.00 a.m. from the *Caronia*:** 'Westbound steamers report bergs, growlers[2] and field ice.'

  Action taken: Captain Smith had message posted on the bridge.

- **At 1.42 p.m. from the *Baltic*:** 'Greek steamer *Athenia* reports passing icebergs and large quantities of field ice.'

  Action taken: Captain Smith showed warning to Ismay, who put it in his pocket and later showed it to other passengers. Finally posted in the chart room at 7.15 p.m.

- **At 1.45 p.m. from the *Amerika*:** 'Passed two large icebergs.'

  Action taken: As this was a private message overheard by the wireless operators, it wasn't sent to the bridge.

2. Growlers are small icebergs rising just a metre or so out of the water; they are named after the sound of trapped air escaping as they melt.

- **At 7.30 p.m. from the *Californian*:** 'Three large bergs five miles to the southward of us.'

  Action taken: Delivered to bridge, but Captain Smith did not know about it as he was in the à la carte restaurant.

- **At 9.40 p.m. from the *Mesaba*:** 'Saw much heavy pack ice and great number large icebergs, also field ice, weather good, clear.'

  Action taken: Never posted on the bridge, as wireless operator Jack Phillips was too busy sending passenger messages, and his assistant Harold Bride was taking a rest.

- **At around 11.00 p.m. from the *Californian*,** just 16 km from the *Titanic*. It was going to say that *Californian* had stopped due to field ice.

  Action taken: Never taken down, as Phillips said he was too busy.

Most passengers had a fairly typical day,[3] and a Sunday service was held in the morning. The lifeboat drill usually held on Sundays was cancelled due to a strong breeze. Though the ice warnings kept on coming, Captain Smith wasn't overly worried. He handed one message to J. Bruce Ismay on his way to lunch. Ismay later showed it to two passengers, Emily Ryerson and Marian Thayer, adding that with luck the *Titanic* might surprise everyone by reaching New York early on Tuesday night.

By now, passengers strolling outside could feel an extra nip in the air. Many stayed indoors, and down in the third-class general room a few off-duty crewmen joined in the dancing. By 7.30 p.m. temperatures were just above freezing. Only a few hardy passengers remained on deck to admire the sunset. It was a gorgeous night. The ocean was flat calm, and though there was no moon, the clear sky was filled with glittering stars. The officers on the bridge were clearly alert to the danger from ice. At 6.00 p.m. Sixth Officer Moody told Second Officer Lightoller he expected the ship to reach ice around 11.00 p.m. Later,

3. One third-class passenger, Alfred Rush, celebrated his 16th birthday and was seen proudly wearing his new pair of long trousers.

First Officer William Murdoch asked a lamp trimmer to close a hatch so its glow wouldn't distract the lookouts up in the crow's nest.[4] When Lightoller returned from dinner, the temperature was dropping rapidly.

Meanwhile Captain Smith was enjoying a dinner party held by millionaire George Widener and his wife Eleanor. Around 8.55 p.m. he went back to the bridge. Lightoller told Smith about the dropping temperatures, adding that though the seas were calm he was confident that the light from the stars would allow the lookouts to spot any icebergs. Smith replied that if the weather got hazy they should slow down, then retired to his cabin at 9.20 p.m.[5] Some ten minutes later, Lightoller asked Moody to instruct the lookouts to 'keep a sharp lookout for ice, particularly small ice and growlers'. The *Titanic* steamed on at full speed, its lights blazing in the darkness.

4. No sonar or radar devices were available at this time. The freezing cold must have made the lookouts' eyes water, making it hard to see ahead in the inky darkness. Even though the officers on the bridge were expecting to meet a large icefield around 11.00 p.m. – Lightoller reminded Murdoch of the danger when his watch ended at 10.00 – no extra lookouts were posted.

5. Captain Smith's cabin was just behind the bridge, so he could get there very quickly if there was an emergency.

The last supper

This is the first-class menu served on Sunday 14 April, just a few hours before disaster struck:

Hors d'Oeuvre Variés
Oysters

Consommé Olga (a veal stock soup garnished with sturgeon spinal marrow)
Cream of Barley (a soup)

Salmon
Mousseline Sauce
Cucumber

Filets Mignons Lili (prepared with foie gras, artichoke hearts and truffle)
Sauté of Chicken Lyonnaise
Vegetable Marrow Farci (stuffed)

Lamb with Mint Sauce
Roast Duckling with Apple Sauce
Sirloin of Beef with Château Potatoes

Green Peas Creamed Carrots
Boiled Rice
Parmentier of New Potatoes

Punch
Romaine

Roasted Squab (young pigeon) on Cress
Cold Asparagus Vinaigrette
Pâté de Foie Gras (goose liver pâté)
Celery

Waldorf Pudding
(the recipe for this has been lost)
Peaches in Chartreuse Jelly
Chocolate and Vanilla Eclairs
French Ice Cream

Second-class dinners were far more straightforward. Passengers were offered a starter of soup and a main course with several choices of meats and vegetables, then finished with puddings such as tapioca pudding and apple tart, ice creams, and fruit and cheese for dessert.

The Sunday third-class 'tea' included roast beef, potatoes and pickles, apricots, fresh bread and butter, and currant buns. Gruel was also served for supper, washed down with beer at 3d (equivalent to 1.25p) a tankard. Kosher meat was offered to Jewish passengers.

Blissfully unaware of the looming icefield, first-class passengers were entertained by concerts while a London vicar led a hundred second-class passengers in the hymn 'For Those in Peril on the Sea'. Around 10 o'clock the lights were turned off in the third-class general room. Many passengers were already heading for their cabins. A few night owls went for a stroll on deck or played a last hand of cards in the first-class smoking room. By 11.00 p.m. most passengers were in bed and a hush descended over the ship, apart from the gentle vibration of the engines. The air outside was close to freezing – cold enough to keep Molly Brown, for one, awake in her bunk.

Inside the wireless room, however, the heat was on. Contact had already been made with the Cape Race station in Canada, and the lone operator Jack Phillips was swamped by demands to send private messages.[6] When a nearby ship, the *Californian*, tried to send another ice warning, 'We are stopped and

6. His assistant, Harold Bride, was taking a well-earned break and was due back at his post at 2.00 a.m. The radio transmitter had broken down just before midnight on Friday 12 April and the two men had worked through the night to fix the problem. This was done by Saturday morning, but by now both men were exhausted and there was a huge backlog of messages.

surrounded by ice,' it was so close that the message blurted into the ears of the already frazzled Phillips. Without waiting for the warning to come through, he angrily tapped back at the *Californian*'s radio operator Cyril Evans: 'Shut up, shut up. I am busy. I am working Cape Race.' After clearing his backlog Phillips tried to apologise, asking Evans to repeat the message, but Evans (the only operator on the *Californian*) had shut down his transmitter and retired for the night.

Around 11.30 p.m. lookouts Frederick Fleet and Reginald Lee noticed a slight haze dead ahead. Perched high above the deck in the freezing cold, they were probably thinking about the warm cabin that would greet them in 20 minutes when their watch ended. Then Fleet spied a pale shape looming out of the darkness ahead. It could only be one thing…

Fleet burst into action, yanking the warning bell in the crow's nest three times. He then telephoned the bridge: 'Iceberg right ahead.'[7]

7. Why didn't they spot it before? As the sea was so calm there were no waves splashing against the base of the iceberg, and there was no moonlight to reflect off it. Moreover, the lookouts had no binoculars – they thought (mistakenly) they had been left at Southampton.

The wireless wonder

In 1912, sending or receiving a wireless message in the middle of the Atlantic was tremendously exciting. In the first four days of the voyage, almost 250 messages or 'Marconigrams' were sent, despite the exorbitant cost of sending a message – a minimum of $3 for just 10 words (as much as many workers earned in a day).

The *Titanic* carried the most powerful wireless equipment in use. Four wire aerials were hung between the masts, and the 5-kilowatt generator gave the Marconi system a range of 560 km during the day and over 1,600 km at night.[8] During sea trials, Jack Phillips exchanged messages with the island of Tenerife in the Canaries, over 3,200 km away.

Passengers delivered their handwritten messages to the inquiry office, and these were sent to the radio room by pneumatic tube. Incoming messages were typed onto a telegram form and sent via pneumatic tube, then hand-delivered to passengers. Navigation messages were delivered directly to the bridge.

The chief Marconi wireless operator was 25-year-old Jack Phillips, assisted by Harold

8. For the technically minded: the reason for the extra range at night is that some radio waves are reflected by the upper atmosphere. During the day, more radio waves are absorbed in the lower atmosphere as it is ionised by sunlight, so they do not reach the upper regions.

Bride, aged 22. For most of the voyage they worked in alternating shifts of 6 hours, so that the wireless was constantly manned. Jack Phillips was nicknamed 'Sparks' as he could send up to 39 words a minute (most operators could send just 25) using the Morse code system of dots and dashes.

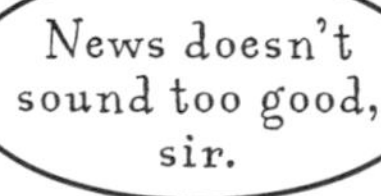

Once the alarm had been given, time must have stood still for the officers on the bridge. Here's what happened next:

1. **Sixth Officer Moody took the call and bellowed the message across to First Officer Murdoch, who had now seen the iceberg for himself and signalled 'full speed astern' to the engine room using the telegraph system.**

2. **At the same time, Murdoch ordered Quartermaster Robert Hichens to turn the wheel 'hard-a-starboard'. This turned the ship to port.**

3. **Once the bow had begun to swing, Murdoch gave a second order, 'hard-a-port', in order to bring the stern around and miss the iceberg completely.**

4. **Murdoch now rang the alarm and flipped the lever that caused the ship's watertight doors to close, down below in the hull.**

Murdoch and Moody had done all they could. They held their breath as the iceberg moved inexorably closer. But a big ship like *Titanic* does not turn quickly, especially when it is slowing down. The lookouts braced themselves for the inevitable collision. At the last second, it looked miraculously as if the giant ship was going to squeeze by without hitting the iceberg. Then, 37 seconds after his warning, Fleet heard a weird scraping sound as the iceberg brushed along the starboard side of the ship. It was 11.40 p.m.

At that moment, the glory of the *Titanic* turned to tragedy.

The iceberg

It's time to meet the villain of the story:

- **Name:** *Iceberg* means 'mountain of ice' in various Germanic languages.

- **Number:** Some 10,000 to 15,000 icebergs break off or 'calve' every year from the Greenland Ice Barrier, but only about 500 of these make it as far south as the North Atlantic shipping lanes.

- **Size:** The iceberg that *Titanic* collided with was around 15–30 m high, and perhaps 60–100 m long. Though a few crew members and passengers saw it, no-one took any photos. Next day, the chief steward of the liner *Prinz Adalbert* photographed an iceberg which had a line of red paint along its base – could this have been the culprit?

- **Danger:** Ice is rock-hard, so hitting an iceberg at speed is like crashing into a vast wall of concrete. To add to the threat, up to 85 per cent of an iceberg lurks underwater.

- **Previous form:** Between 1882 and 1890, 14 liners or merchant ships were lost and 40 seriously damaged due to ice in this part of the North Atlantic (not including the many fishing vessels lost in the area).

Telltale Signs

On a clear day, a big iceberg is hard to miss. On a dark, moonless night, it's a different matter altogether. *Titanic* lookout Archie Jewell claimed: 'You can smell the ice before you get to it.' This is possibly true, as the minerals in icebergs can give off a distinctive smell when they break off. Passenger Elizabeth Shutes, a governess, noted that a weird smell hung in the air that night, like a cave in a Swiss glacier she had once visited.

As the towering wall of ice passed alongside the ship, chunks of ice fell onto the deck. Many passengers slept on, though first-class passenger Henry Sleeper Harper sat up and saw the berg scrape against his window. Another passenger remarked that it felt as though the ship had gone over a thousand marbles. But third-class passengers were thrown out of their beds in the cabins just above the bow cargo holds. Further aft, stokers felt a judder and thought the ship had lost a propeller blade.

Captain Smith was jolted awake and rushed to the bridge. After Murdoch explained what had happened, the two men went out on deck. The sight of the massive iceberg was enough to tell the captain that there could be serious damage to the hull. Back on the bridge, Smith ordered the engines to stop. The ship eventually came to a silent halt. Everything was eerily calm.

A wall of water

Below the surface, the great ship had been fatally wounded. The iceberg had scraped along the side of ship, bending the hull's steel plates so that the rivets popped open below the waterline. Below decks, all hell broke loose. In boiler room No. 6 there was an ominous rumble and a wall of icy water burst in from the side of the ship.[9] Alarm bells warned that the emergency doors were about to shut, and the stokers ran for their lives as the waters began to rise. Two men slipped under the door, while another clambered up the emergency ladder.[10]

9. It's estimated that water poured in at a rate of 8,000 litres a minute.
10. Despite the myths, it's unlikely that any crew members were trapped by the watertight doors, as they could be reopened by hand.

Smith ordered Fourth Officer Boxhall to inspect the forward part of the ship. When Boxhall reappeared just a few minutes later and gave the all clear, the Captain wasn't convinced, and sent him back. This time he met the ship's carpenter, John Hutchinson, who told Boxhall the ship was taking in water. A mail clerk reported that the mail room was filling fast. After seeing the floating mail bags for himself, Boxhall returned to the bridge.

J. Bruce Ismay was woken by the noise of the iceberg grinding against the hull. Slinging his overcoat over his pyjamas, he strode up to the bridge. Smith told him the grim news, then summoned Thomas Andrews – no-one knew the ship better. Andrews explained that *Titanic* was safe as long as only two compartments were flooded.

It soon became clear, however, that the first five compartments in the bow were taking in water. The weight of water in these would pull the head of the vessel down, slowly flooding the other compartments one by one.[11]

11. The walls between the compartments had a gap at the top, so as the ship leaned forward, water sloshed over into the next compartment. So much for the watertight doors!

Mail room

The *Titanic* had a post office on F Deck and a mail storeroom directly below. Some 400,000 letters in 3,364 mailbags were on board, all to be sorted before arriving in New York, along with numerous letters and postcards written by passengers en route. When the mail room began flooding, the five postal workers attempted to drag 200 sacks of registered mail to the upper decks in the hope of saving them. Press-ganging several stewards into helping them, they hauled the soggy sacks (each weighing 45 kg or more) up several flights of stairs. None of the postal workers survived the disaster.

Though the engineering team had desperately rigged hoses to pump out the water, it was an impossible task. The *Titanic* was going to sink, and fast. When Smith asked 'How long have we got?', Andrews replied that the ship was doomed and had no more than two hours left afloat.

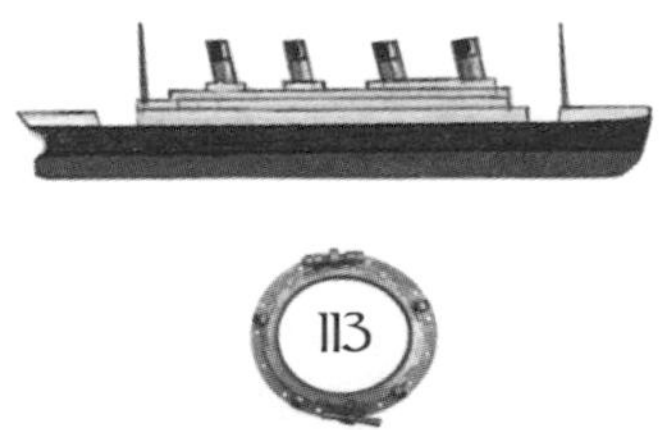

Calls for help

At 12.05 a.m. Smith ordered the crew to wake the passengers and hand out lifejackets. Stewards were given strict orders to do everything very calmly, to avoid creating a panic among the passengers.[12] But in his heart the captain must have known that there were only enough lifeboats for half the people on board, and there was no sign of any ships near enough to give immediate help.

Captain Smith told Fourth Officer Boxhall to work out the ship's position. Boxhall jotted this down – 41.46 N, 50.14 W – and whisked the message to the wireless room. Jack Phillips immediately sent out a distress call. Though there were several ships within range, it was midnight and most radio operators had turned in for the night. Luckily, the wireless operator aboard the Cunard liner RMS *Carpathia*, 21-year-old Harold Cottam, was waiting for a message. Picking up the distress call from *Titanic*, he tapped out: 'Shall I tell my

12. To keep the passengers calm, no general alarm was ever sounded and many of the crew were given no instructions. As a result, a quiet chaos ruled in which few realised the grave danger they were in, so passengers were very slow to head for the lifeboats.

captain? Do you require assistance?' To which Phillips replied: 'Yes. Come quick!'

Soon the *Carpathia* was steaming at full speed towards the *Titanic*. But the ship was 93 km away; it would take almost four hours to reach the sinking liner. Knowing that every minute counted, the commander of the *Carpathia,* Captain Rostron, ordered the entire crew to be mustered. By pushing the engines to the limit, he increased the ship's speed to almost 18 knots (33.4 km/h).

Save Our Souls?

At the time, all ships were given three-letter call signs in Morse code. At first, Jack Phillips sent out the distress call CQD – a general call to other ships in the area – followed by MGY, *Titanic*'s call sign. Phillips later sent out an SOS, and was one of the first operators to do so (the first to use it was Cunard liner SS *Slavonia*, wrecked off the Azores in June 1909). Harold Bride joked: 'It's the new call, and it may be your last chance to send it.' SOS is easy to recognise in Morse code: 'dot-dot-dot, dash-dash-dash, dot-dot-dot' (. . . – – – . . .) – it doesn't stand for 'Save Our Souls' (or anything else) as is sometimes said.

Back on the *Titanic,* there was already a stream of third-class passengers flowing from the bows to the stern, many carrying all their belongings. They had been jolted awake by the collision, while first- and second-class passengers on the upper decks were only slowly beginning to realise something was up. A few ventured on deck to see what was going on. They knew the ship had stopped, but not much more. The beautiful starry night and calm sea only added to their sense of security.

Many of the stewards were equally in the dark. They calmly assured passengers the ship would soon be under way again. Though rumours began to spread that the ship had struck an iceberg, few took the news seriously. After all, the *Titanic* was unsinkable. Thomas Andrews was one of the few staff telling passengers to put on their lifejackets with any sense of urgency. Though there was already a very gentle slant towards the bows, the ship was still steady. Many passengers still didn't really believe the *Titanic* was going to sink. Others were driven back inside by the cold air or the deafening roar of excess steam being released from the boilers.

The Doubters

- One story tells how a group of passengers were asked to move to one side of the ship to stop it tilting over. Four men playing bridge took a quick look over the rail and calmly went back to their cards. They just didn't realise the danger.

- Seventeen-year-old Jack Thayer and his father watched as a group of boys happily played football with chunks of ice on the stern deck. One of the second-class passengers is said to have suggested using chunks of ice from thc iceberg in their drinks, while Edith Rosenbaum Russell later remembered having a snowball fight with other passengers: 'We thought it was fun.'

- One female passenger was heard crying out: 'What do they need of lifeboats? This ship could smash a hundred icebergs and not feel it.'

- Hudson J. Allison was heard scolding Sarah Daniels, his wife's maid, saying: 'You're nervous, go back to bed! The ship can't sink.'

- Third-class passenger Daniel Buckley got out of his bunk to find himself standing in a pool of water. When he warned other passengers, they laughed and told him to go back to sleep.

- Karl Howard Behr later described how many passengers reacted: 'Ismay walked over to us and calmly told us we should get into a lifeboat... The prospect of being lowered some 80 feet [24 m] or more into the ocean in the dark was not alluring [attractive]... no-one therefore moved to obey Ismay as he walked off.'
- When the stewards knocked on their doors and warned passengers of the danger, some simply ignored them and stayed in their beds.

Deep in the ship, it was a very different story. By midnight, water was entering the squash courts on F and G decks. In the engine room, Second Engineer James Hesketh was terrified that the boilers were going to blow up. He ordered cold water to be pumped into the fireboxes. A mix of steam and ash poured out, enveloping the firemen in hot smog. Yet the *Titanic* was so long that many of the stokers near the stern still didn't realise the ship was flooding. The electrical generators were above the waterline, so everything seemed to be working as normal.

Abandon Ship!

Because there had been no drills, there was chaos on deck as crew members simply manned the nearest lifeboat. It was all very bizarre, with the orchestra playing breezy ragtime tunes while the lifeboats were readied and passengers wandered about on deck half-dressed. Some returned to their cabins to put on warmer clothes. A queue formed outside the Purser's office as wealthy passengers demanded the return of their valuables.

Even though he knew soon after midnight that the ship was going down and the *Carpathia* wouldn't arrive in time, Captain Smith waited until 12.25 a.m. before giving the order to start loading the boats. The crew followed the age-old rule of 'women and children first'. On the port side, Second Officer Lightoller was even stricter – he insisted it was women and children only, and famously stopped John Jacob Astor, one of the richest men in the world, from joining his pregnant wife Madeleine.[13]

13. Lightoller even refused to let 11-year-old Willie Coutts into a lifeboat, as his straw hat made him look older; and Billy Carter only made it after his mother put her hat on him so he looked like a girl.

Around 12.45 a.m. the first few lifeboats were lowered into the water. The 18-metre drop to the sea petrified passengers who thought they might be jolted into the icy sea below.[14] Amazingly, many of the first lifeboats were launched half-full,[15] partly because passengers still didn't believe the ship was sinking and didn't fancy the idea of bobbing about in the middle of the Atlantic in a rowing boat. Ship's baker Charles Joughin even tried to shove unwilling passengers into the lifeboats, and heroically gave up his own place on Lifeboat No. 10.

As the water rose through the ship, more and more passengers appeared on deck. Many third-class passengers didn't speak English, so it was hard to explain the women-and-children-first rule. Even when they did understand, many families refused to be split up. Captain Smith, sensing a growing panic, decided to arm his officers.

14. As Lifeboat No. 5 was lowered, a crew member shouted, 'Make sure the plug is in!' – a reminder to plug the hole in the bottom of the keel that was used to drain water when the boat was stored on deck.
15. The first boat to be lowered, Lifeboat No. 7, had just 27 people on board when it could hold up to 65.

Around this time, the lights of another ship were sighted by several passengers, including Colonel Archibald Gracie. They were going to be saved! Fourth Officer Boxhall guessed the lights were just 8 km away, but, despite his repeated attempts to flash a message using a signal lamp, there was no reply. A frustrated Boxhall ordered Quartermaster George Rowe to bring the emergency rockets to the bridge – their last hope of attracting attention. At 12.55 a.m. the first white distress flare soared 240 m into the night sky and exploded in a shower of white stars. Seven more rockets were fired at 5-minute intervals.[16]

The sight of the rockets was enough to make many passengers realise that they were in big trouble and no help was coming. Meanwhile the bow was sinking lower and lower into the water. There were tragic scenes on deck as women were separated from their husbands and children. The air rang with the screams of people crying out for their loved ones.

16. The last of the rockets was seen by Chief Officer Stone on the Californian. *At this time there was no internationally recognised distress signal, so he thought it was probably a firework display, common on the big liners. Nonetheless, he still reported what he had seen to his captain. Stone was ordered to signal by lamp, but his message was never picked up by the* Titanic.

The band played on

To calm the passengers, bandmaster Wallace Hartley led his seven musicians in playing cheery music and ultimately the hymn 'Abide with Me' until the water came up to their knees (though Harold Bride could have sworn the final tune he heard was the popular waltz 'Autumn'). Perhaps the music gave the passengers a false sense of security, but no-one can doubt the bravery of the band members. None survived.

The orchestra moved out onto the open deck, but the music was no longer enough to calm the increasing desperate passengers. By 1.30 a.m. the ship was slanting so badly that tables and chairs starting sliding down the deck. As people realised there were not enough lifeboats on board, a real sense of panic set in.

From the lower decks came the screams of trapped third-class passengers. They probably weren't deliberately locked in, but Colonel Archibald Gracie and others later reported that they saw a mass of passengers from

steerage pouring on deck just before the ship went down. Though stewards had been sent downstairs to guide the women and children to the lifeboats, the men may have been told to stay down below until late on. If they did attempt to head upstairs, they would have been left to find their own way through the maze of passages.

Up on deck, people sobbed and cried. Officers did their best to hold back the panicking passengers. As Lifeboat No. 14 was launched, some even tried to jump in from the rails. Fifth Officer Lowe fired three warning shots with his revolver, and the crowd backed off. Captain Smith refused to leave his ship and stayed on deck with hundreds of other men who watched as the lifeboats rowed away. There was nothing anyone could do but wait for the ship to sink.

The good, the bad and the ugly

Around the ship, all kinds of dramas were being played out:

- One of the first officers to die, engineer Jonathan Shepherd, broke his leg falling down a manhole in the flooded boiler room No. 5. His colleague Herbert Harvey gallantly tried to save him, but both men drowned.
- Several women stubbornly refused to leave their husbands, most famously Ida Straus, who said: 'I've always stayed with my husband, so why should I leave him now? We have been living together for many years. Where you go, I go.' She and her husband Isidor then sat and watched in a pair of deck chairs before returning to their cabin, where they hugged each other as the rising water flooded the room.
- Two seamen dragged Mrs Charlotte Collyer from her husband Harvey. As she was carried away kicking and screaming, her husband cried out: 'Go, Lottie! For God's sake, be brave and go!'
- One woman slipped as she clambered into a lifeboat and would have plunged to her death if a sailor had not grabbed her ankles and hauled her back into the boat with help from others.

- The cables on Lifeboat No. 14 jammed as it was lowered. Seaman Joseph Scarrott stopped it from tipping over by cutting the cables with a knife. Thankfully the boat was close to the water, so no-one was hurt as it fell the last few feet.

- Ruth Becker got separated from her family after being sent by her mother to collect blankets from their cabin. A sailor shoved her into Lifeboat No. 13, still clutching the two blankets. These were chopped up and given to a group of shivering stokers who were still wearing the shorts and vests suited to the fierce heat of the boiler rooms.

- In the midst of the crisis, some still found time for humour. One man joked as he fastened a lifejacket onto Mrs Vera Dick: 'Try this on. They're the very latest thing this season. Everyone is wearing them now!'

- When Colonel Archibald Gracie bumped into Fred Wright, the ship's squash coach, he cancelled their appointment for 7.30 a.m. – knowing the squash court was already flooded!

- Having put his mistress safely on a lifeboat, millionaire Benjamin Guggenheim and his valet headed back to their cabin to dress in their finest evening suits, then returned to the top deck. Guggenheim told another passenger that he wouldn't dream of using his power and fame to win a place in a lifeboat:

'Never forget that Benjamin Guggenheim died like a gentleman.'

- Thomas Andrews was seen and heard helping passengers everywhere, but, overcome by guilt, he decided to go down with the ship. He was last seen in the first-class lounge, refusing to put on his lifejacket.

- By contrast, White Star boss J. Bruce Ismay was such a nuisance during the launching of the lifeboats that Fifth Officer Lowe ordered him to go away. He was also happy to board Collapsible Lifeboat C, one of the last to be launched, while other men stood back, ready to die. In the weeks that followed, Ismay's reputation was savaged in a vicious campaign by newspapers owned by his enemy William Randolph Hearst. They asked: 'Who would not rather die a hero than live a coward?' In fact, several male survivors were branded cowards for surviving when so many other men had died.

- Sir Cosmo and Lady Duff Gordon were also slated by the newspapers after it emerged that Sir Cosmo had offered £5 to the crew on his lifeboat not to go back and pick up any survivors. Duff claimed the £5 was for the crew to buy new kit back in England – but few swallowed his story.

- Some crew thought only of saving themselves, such as Paul Maugé, the kitchen clerk in the Ritz restaurant, who leapt into a boat as it was lowered (another member of the crew tried to pull Maugé out as the boat passed him on a lower deck). When the two wireless operators left their posts just 10 minutes before the ship went down, they found a stoker trying to steal Harold Bride's lifejacket. They knocked him unconscious and headed out on deck.

- One male passenger broke a woman's ribs by leaping into a lifeboat.

- Edward Ryan wrapped a shawl around his shoulders and head to make him look like a woman – probably not the only male passenger to do this. He then grabbed a girl who was standing nearby, and jumped with her 9 metres into a boat.

What would you take?

- As Adolf Dyker helped his wife into the lifeboat with a cheery 'I'll see you later,' he handed her a satchel with two gold watches, two diamond rings, a sapphire necklace and 200 Swedish crowns.
- Fashion writer Edith Rosenbaum Russell took only her toy pig, Maxine. She wound the pig's tail and it played music to drown out the cries of those in the water.
- Divinity student Sidney Stuart Collett kept his Bible, and Lawrence Beesley stuffed his jacket pockets with books.
- Norman Chambers took a revolver and a compass; steward James Johnson chose four oranges.
- Mrs Helen Bishop left $11,000 in jewellery, but sent her husband back for her muff.
- Major Arthur Peuchen left behind $200,000 in bonds and $100,000 in stocks. He chose warm clothes instead.
- Hudson J. Allison was weighed down with keys, letters, photos, three pocket diaries, a railway ticket book, two pocket books, a card case, $143 in notes and $4.40 in coins, a chain with insurance medals, £15 in gold, a $100 Thomas Cook & Sons travellers' cheque, £35 in notes, gold cufflinks, a diamond solitaire ring, a gold stud, a knife, a silver tie clip and a traveller's ticket.

Some passengers flung deck chairs, doors and trunks overboard to make rafts. At the rear of the boat deck, Father Thomas Byles said a few final prayers. One group went to the smoking room to play a last hand of cards, while tennis player R. Norris Williams and his father went to the gym to warm themselves up on the exercise bicycles.

As the waters rose up the bows, there were last-ditch efforts on deck to free Collapsible Lifeboat B, but it was swept overboard by a large wave. Around 2.15 a.m. the last lifeboat, Collapsible A, was cut free after the lines snagged, though it too was swamped by a wave. In the chaos, George Rheims and Eugene Daly reported later that they saw First Officer Murdoch shoot a passenger near Collapsible A and then shoot himself in the head with his revolver.[17] In the wireless room, the messages grew increasingly desperate: 'We're sinking fast.' At 1.45 a.m. the *Carpathia* received a final report stating: 'Engine room full up to boilers.'[18]

17. Lightoller, when questioned afterwards, swore this did not happen.
18. A faint message was apparently heard by the Canadian liner SS Virginian *as late as 2.17 a.m.*

Even as late as 2.10 a.m., Chief Engineer Joseph Bell and his team were still working in the depths of the ship, making sure her lights kept shining until the last moment. By the time they arrived on deck, all the lifeboats were gone. Without their determination, the ship would have been plunged into darkness and many more would have died in the confusion. Around 2.18 a.m., the *Titanic*'s lights flickered one last time, then went out for good.

By now, the bows had sunk so far underwater that an enormous wave surged up the deck, sweeping many passengers into the sea. The forward funnel snapped, smashing down on dozens of swimmers in the water, and shortly afterwards the *Titanic*'s stern began to rise out of the sea. Some grabbed the railings and hung on for dear life; others, losing their grip, tumbled into the water below. There was a tremendous crashing sound as anything that wasn't bolted to the floor tumbled forward.

The *Titanic*'s colossal boilers ripped away from the hull and crashed through the ship with a terrible roar. Soon after there was an almighty cracking sound as the hull broke in half.

The forward half vanished into the dark water. On the way down the pressure of water created a series of explosions, releasing large pockets of air.

The stern settled back into the water for a short while, then tilted up almost vertically into the night sky for a brief moment before it too disappeared beneath the waves at 2.20 a.m. Now the surface of the sea was calm again, the silence broken by the shouts and cries of those in the water. Some 30 men swam to the upturned Collapsible B and scrambled aboard, including Second Officer Lightoller, but one false move and the boat was likely to flip over and sink. Another dozen men clambered onto Collapsible A.

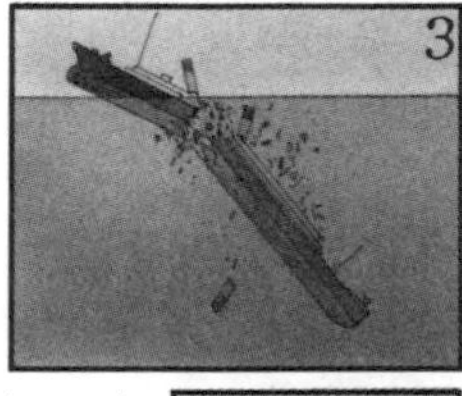

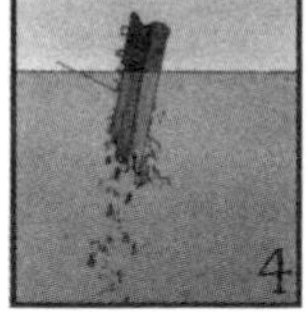

1. Watertight compartments begin to fill.
2. Forward funnel collapses.
3. Hull breaks in two and bow section sinks.
4. Stern section sinks.

Saved by a miracle

- Baker Charles Joughin dragged himself aboard Collapsible B after spending an incredible two hours in the water. Don't believe the stories that say he was saved by being drunk, as, though alcohol does give a feeling of warmth, in reality it helps heat to leave the body.

- Though no-one seems to have survived by clinging to the wreckage, second-class passenger Emile Portaluppi claimed he escaped by temporarily hanging on to a floating cake of ice until a lifeboat picked him up.

- Colonel Archibald Gracie jumped from the top deck and was sucked down with the *Titanic*. Then, in his own words, he was 'propelled by some great force through the water. This might have been occasioned by explosions under the water, and I remembered fearful stories of people being boiled to death... I had the greatest difficulty in holding my breath until I came to the surface. There was nothing in sight save the ocean, dotted with ice and strewn with large masses of wreckage. Dying men and women all about me were groaning and crying piteously. By moving from one piece of wreckage to another, at last I reached a cork raft.' (This was Collapsible Lifeboat B.)

- Wireless operator Harold Bride found himself trapped below Collapsible B. He knew he had just one chance of survival. Taking a large breath from the air trapped beneath the boat, he kicked for the surface and climbed aboard.

- Two small dogs, a Pomeranian and a Pekinese, were taken aboard lifeboats and rescued with their owners. There's also the notorious story of Rigel, a black Newfoundland dog said to have saved the lives of several survivors by barking up to the rescue ship *Carpathia*. This shaggy dog story was probably made up by Jonas Briggs, who also lied that he was a seaman aboard the *Carpathia*.

- In another colourful but probably untrue story, a famous gambler and conman nicknamed 'Titanic Thompson' was said to have escaped from the sinking ship by dressing in women's clothes, along with two other gamblers, 'Doc Owen' and 'Kid Homer'.[19] Once in the lifeboat, which was packed mainly with emigrant women, they took off their disguises. Supposedly no-one minded, since men were needed to row the boat.

19. Though the disguise story may not be true, Kid Homer was a real passenger (and gambler), who boarded under the name E. Haven and was rescued in Lifeboat 15.

Nearly 1,500 people were now in the water, kept afloat by their lifejackets. But few can survive floating in freezing water for longer than 30 minutes, and the *Carpathia* was still an hour away. The lifeboats had rowed away from the *Titanic* to avoid being sucked under as she sank. Many had empty seats. Though Captain Smith had given orders that they should go back and rescue as many as they could from the water, most lifeboats stayed put. Would you have gone back? Most occupants were too selfish, or too afraid that they would be swamped by swimmers trying to haul themselves aboard.

Just one lifeboat, No. 14, commanded by Fifth Officer Harold Lowe, went back to help. Nine people were pulled from the water (though three of them later died). Few of the survivors in the lifeboats ever forgot the horrible cries and groans of the dying. But by 3.00 a.m. all that remained was a terrible, deathly hush.

In cold blood?

Though the official inquiry gave the cause of death as drowning, most victims – even good swimmers – were probably killed by the freezing water in just a few minutes. They would have been paralysed by 'cold shock', which can cause a heart attack. Others in the water were sucked under as the ship sank below the waves, while a few may have died from a broken neck, having jumped from a great height with the heavy lifejacket strapped to them.

A dignified end

We've dressed in our best and are prepared to go down like gentlemen.

Benjamin Guggenheim
1865–1912

Millionaire Benjamin Guggenheim and his valet, Victor Giglio, had taken off their lifebelts and put on evening dress, knowing there would be no escape from the sinking ship.

Cometh the hour...

Captain Rostron of the *Carpathia* steams to the rescue

CHAPTER FIVE

THE TOWN THAT SANK

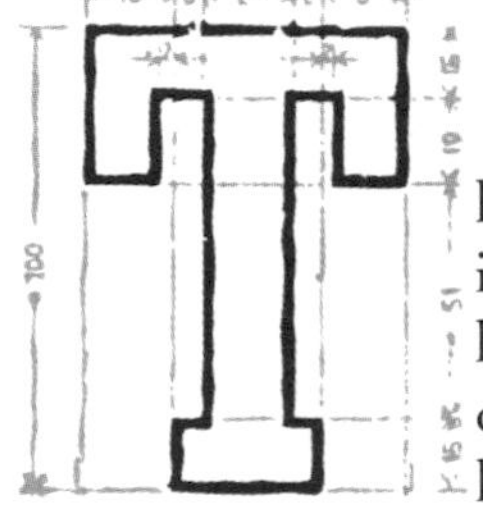

he *Titanic* was gone. Those in the first lifeboats to be launched had watched for over an hour as little by little the brightly lit ship sank below the waves. Others couldn't bear to look, like J. Bruce Ismay in Collapsible C, who turned his back on his dream ship as it slowly disappeared from sight.

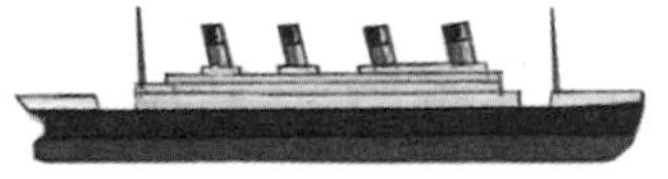

The mystery ship

Many passengers clearly saw lights from another vessel that never came to help. It was so close that Captain Smith is said to have ordered lifeboat crews to drop passengers off with this ship and come back for more. But which ship was it?

The US Senate pointed the finger at the *Californian*, a merchant vessel sailing from London to Boston. The *Californian*'s captain, Stanley Lord, claimed his men tried to signal a distant ship with a flashing Morse lamp, which had a range of 16 km, but got no response. Later, Second Officer Herbert Stone and other members of the crew saw all eight distress rockets fired by the *Titanic*, but didn't try to get in touch by wireless. Strange atmospheric conditions may have confused both Captain Lord and passengers on the *Titanic*, making the lights on the other ship appear much closer than they really were.

There may have been a third ship nearby, a Norwegian sailing boat called the *Samson*, which was illegally hunting seals in the area. According to the diary of First Officer Henrik Naess, the *Samson*'s crew saw the *Titanic*'s distress rockets, but hurried away as they were afraid they might have been fired from a US coastguard ship. However, if the ship's logs are correct, the *Samson* was actually over 2,000 km away in another part of the North Atlantic!

Out of more than 2,200 passengers, just 712 survived the sinking. As they sat shivering in the lifeboats, there was no certainty that they would be rescued. It was dark and chaotic – one baby was almost hurled overboard when it was mistaken for a bundle of clothing. Mercifully, it was saved at the last second when it began bawling. Though the lifeboats were stocked with a water tank and beaker, tins of biscuits and lights, in most cases these were forgotten about by the crew and no-one discovered them.

For the children, it must have been particularly terrifying. Parents did their best to cheer them up by pointing out shooting stars or singing songs, while Edith Rosenbaum Russell entertained others on her boat with her musical pig. Some boats tried to signal for help, especially when they glimpsed the dim lights of another ship on the horizon. Emily Goldsmith set her straw hat on fire, while Ella White waved a cane with a built-in electric light.

The Unsinkable Molly Brown

As the *Titanic* was sinking, millionairess Margaret Brown had sensibly put on seven pairs of stockings for warmth and grabbed her lucky Egyptian statuette as she left her cabin. Later, she was one of the 26 women on board Lifeboat No. 6, commanded by Quartermaster Robert Hichens. Hichens refused to order his boat to row back and help the survivors in the water, saying, 'It is our lives now, not theirs.' Mrs Brown was furious – and when Hichens refused to row towards the *Carpathia* she threatened to throw him overboard. She rallied the other women and encouraged them to start rowing, if only to keep warm. Hichens began throwing insults at her, but no-one took any notice. Molly Brown was in charge, and her steely resolve was later celebrated in books, movies and even a musical, *The Unsinkable Molly Brown*.

Help comes at last

Meanwhile the *Carpathia* raced through the dark towards the *Titanic*. Its commander, Captain Arthur Rostron,[1] was well aware of the risk from the ice and so he posted several extra lookouts. Below decks, his crew got ready to receive the survivors, though they had no idea how many to expect.[2] Three dining rooms were turned into first-aid rooms, with blankets, hot soup, tea and brandy at the ready.

When the *Carpathia* finally neared the *Titanic*'s last reported position, around 3.30 a.m. (an hour after the ship had gone down), Rostron feared the worst. In the gloom he couldn't see any sign of the ship or even any wreckage. He decided to cut the engines, as it was safer for any surviving lifeboats to come to him. The *Carpathia* began firing rockets every 15 minutes, and on seeing these the survivors madly waved and shouted. They also burned

1. His crew called him 'the electric spark' because of his energy and quick thinking.
2. The Carpathia, *which belonged to the rival Cunard Line, could carry 2,550 people but on this voyage only 743 passengers were on board, so there was plenty of room for the* Titanic *survivors.*

newspapers, letters and handkerchiefs to attract attention. Despite this, it was another 40 minutes before the first lifeboat was sighted in the water by the light of one of the green flares. In it were Fourth Officer Boxhall and 24 other survivors.

Over the next few hours all the survivors were taken on board the *Carpathia*. The first to clamber aboard was heiress Elizabeth Allen, around 4.10 a.m. Fourth Officer Boxhall came up to the bridge and confirmed what Rostron already knew: the *Titanic* had sunk at 2.20 a.m. By now the sun was rising and the survivors could see the giant ice field stretching north. Rostron realised he needed to move fast, as most of the those in the lifeboats had been out in the open for 4 or 5 hours and were wet through and exhausted. The wind had picked up and the sea was getting increasingly choppy.

Worst off were those on Collapsible B, still some 6 km away from the *Carpathia*, upturned and close to sinking. Second Officer Lightoller had ordered the survivors on board to stand upright to balance the boat as the waves rocked it back and forth. As things turned from bad to worse, Lightoller blew his whistle, and in the nick of time two other lifeboats came to the rescue.

When the lifeboats drew up alongside the *Carpathia*, some survivors were strong enough to scramble up the rope ladder. Others, weak from exhaustion or cold, were winched up on bosuns' chairs, sacks, and cargo nets. All in all, it took over four hours to pick up the survivors as they were scattered over a wide area. Last aboard the *Carpathia* was Second Officer Lightoller from Lifeboat No. 12, the most senior officer to survive.

The bedraggled survivors were given hot drinks and dry clothing, some donated by the *Carpathia*'s passengers. While some were taken to cabins, others huddled on deck dressed in a curious mix of nightclothes, evening gowns and fur coats; some were still wrapped in blankets. There was an eerie silence on board, broken by the odd cry or moan – it was all just too ghastly to talk about. Many survivors had lost family or friends, and scoured the *Carpathia* for their loved ones.

Though there were a few happy reunions,[3] most suffered the agony of lost husbands, sons and fathers.

When the last of *Titanic*'s lifeboats had been winched aboard, Rostron ordered the *Carpathia* to make a final search of the area where the ship went down. He held out little hope – no human could survive 6 hours in the icy waters. A memorial service was held in the main lounge to distract passengers while the search was carried out. No-one was found. Then the *Carpathia*'s officers got on with the grim task of drawing up the list of survivors. This was broadcast by Harold Cottam and Harold Bride in the wireless room, along with a stream of private messages to family and friends.

3. 12-year-old Ruth Becker found her family again, and four women were reunited with their husbands on the Carpathia.

Read *all* about it!

News of the disaster was already spreading around the globe. By Monday morning many newspapers were carrying the story, but confusion was rife:

ALL SAVED FROM TITANIC AFTER COLLISION... LINER IS BEING TOWED TO HALIFAX
New York Evening Sun, 15 April

PASSENGERS SAFELY MOVED AND STEAMER TITANIC TAKEN IN TOW
Christian Science Monitor, 15 April

TITANIC SUNK, NO LIVES LOST
Daily Mail, 16 April

White Star themselves only learned the truth at 6.20 p.m. on 15 April in a telegram from the *Olympic*, which was confirmed by the *Carpathia* two hours later. Early the next morning, a handwritten list of survivors was posted outside the offices of the *New York Times*.

The sinking became legendary because of the *Titanic*'s 'unsinkable' reputation, the crowd of celebrities on board, and the growing use of the telegraph and photographs to report stories quickly and dramatically. But these modern devices didn't stop newspapers from printing glaringly inaccurate stories, such as:

CAPTAIN SMITH A SUICIDE
Los Angeles Times, 19 April

Home

Once free of the deadly ice field, it took three days for the *Carpathia* to return to New York. Already traumatised by the sinking, Karl Behr wasn't the only survivor on board who got a fright when a storm broke out on Tuesday night, mistaking thunder and lightning for another collision. Most survivors were still in a state of shock, but as the full horror of the tragedy slowly sank in, dozens of women sat in groups and comforted each other as they wept at the loss of their menfolk.[4]

On the evening of Thursday 18 April the *Carpathia* arrived in New York. She was met by a thick fog, thundery skies, and a fleet of small boats packed with anxious relatives and with reporters hungry for horror stories and tales of derring-do.[5] The ship

4. Not everyone was so caring: one survivor, Alfred Nourney (travelling under the false name of 'Baron von Drachstedt'), snuck off and made a comfy bed for himself by hoarding a pile of blankets meant for other survivors. He was discovered by an irate young woman who whipped the blankets away, saying 'And to think that such as you were saved!'

5. Reporter Carlos F. Hurd, a passenger on the Carpathia, *stole a march on the press pack by interviewing survivors on board (though he still found time to look after orphan Edmond Navratil). On arrival in New York he flung his story in a parcel to a colleague who had come alongside in a tug hired by the* New York World.

headed first for the White Star piers to return the *Titanic*'s lifeboats. The boats were soon overrun by souvenir hunters who stripped them of lifejackets, nameplates, numberplates, oars and even blankets.

The *Carpathia* then docked at the Cunard pier. Here a scrum of photographers and a crowd of 30,000 lined up along the docks, lit by spotlights so the survivors could pick out their relatives. As the first of the *Titanic*'s weary passengers walked across the gangway into the pier buildings, around 9.30 p.m., the tension in the crowd grew. Cameras flashed and people pushed and shoved to get a better view. To add to the hysteria, only now did some find out that their relatives had gone down with the ship.

Some survivors were taken to hospital where they were treated for frostbite, broken bones or shock. Others were booked into hotels or taken home by their relatives. Though at first local immigration charities looked after many of the 174 survivors from third class, within a few days many found themselves in a strange city without money or a place to stay.

Recovering the dead

On Wednesday 17 April the cable repair ship *Mackay-Bennett* set sail from Halifax, Nova Scotia, the first of four ships chartered by the White Star Line to recover as many bodies as possible from the North Atlantic. The grisly job had to be done as quickly as possible before currents swept them away, or attacks from birds and other sea life made the bodies impossible to identify. By Saturday 20 April the *Mackay-Bennett* had arrived in an area where dead bodies had been seen floating the day after the disaster.

Over the next week the *Mackay-Bennett* recovered 190 bodies. The ship didn't have enough chemicals to preserve them all, so the captain decided to embalm only the first-class passengers. The other 116 bodies were buried at sea, sewn in canvas and weighed down with iron bars. Even so, the *Mackay-Bennett* was so heavily laden with bodies it had to return to Halifax, the base for the recovery operation.

☆

What happened to the missing bodies?

- **Swept away?** Many bodies just got lost in the ocean's vastness – the sea is remarkably quick to obliterate all traces of a disaster.
- **Sunk?** Most victims were found floating in an upright position, propped up by their lifejackets. Having died from the cold, they looked as though they were asleep. However, some bodies may have sunk after a few days as lifejackets and lungs filled with water.
- **Decomposed?** Dead bodies are eaten from the inside out by bacteria escaping from the intestines. After 10 hours, gases caused by this process make bodies float, after which they sink again for good.
- **Nibbled?** If a body sinks quickly to the bottom, the cold there prevents the bacteria from going to work, so the corpse remains in good condition. On the seabed, fish, eels and crabs eat the soft tissues, or else the flesh slowly turns into fatty 'grave wax'. Soon all that's left is the skeleton, and over about 75 years even this dissolves in the surrounding water.
- **Adrift?** An unlikely story reported in the *New York World* (26 April 1912) described how the crew of the German ship *Prinzess Irene* saw a group of survivors huddled together and frozen to death on an iceberg, some 80 km from the site of the sinking.

The *Minia*, which replaced the *Mackay-Bennett*, found a further 17 bodies. Another ship, the *Montmagny*, recovered three more, while over the next month other ships came across four bodies. Three of these were found by the RMS *Oceanic* aboard Collapsible Lifeboat A, which had drifted several kilometres from the wreck site (these victims were already dead when the other survivors on board were transferred to Lifeboat 14).

In Halifax a temporary morgue was set up. The bodies were labelled and any possessions found on them were placed in small canvas bags, numbered to match the body number. Forty-nine identified bodies were shipped out to families and buried elsewhere, while the remaining 150 were buried in three different local cemeteries, a long way from their homes and families.[6] Starting on 3 May, the burials took over a month. A local official wrote to families all over the world. The port of Southampton, where many of the crew lived, was hardest hit. On one street alone, one in every 20 families lost a relative in the disaster.

6. The three cemeteries in Halifax where you can still see the graves of Titanic *victims are the Fairview Lawn Cemetery (121 victims), the Baron de Hirsch Cemetery (10) and the Mount Olivet Cemetery (19).*

The unknown

Around half the bodies recovered after the sinking were never formally identified, so just the body number and the inscription 'DIED APRIL 15, 1912' were placed on their graves. However, experts have a good idea who some of them are, from details such as their hair colour, their clothing or the coins in their pockets.

For decades, no-one knew the identity of the 'unknown child', a fair-haired baby boy recovered by the *Mackay-Bennett*. Then, 90 years after the tragedy, in 2002, DNA tests appeared to match the body to a family from Finland. Five years later, however, further tests revealed that the child was in fact 19-month-old Sidney Leslie Goodwin, one of a family of eight from Melksham in Wiltshire, England, who all died when the ship went down.

His epitaph reads:

ERECTED
TO THE MEMORY
OF AN
UNKNOWN CHILD
WHOSE REMAINS
WERE RECOVERED
AFTER THE
DISASTER TO
THE "TITANIC"
APRIL 15TH 1912

Aftermath and inquiry

When the first wireless messages came in on Monday 15 April, the general manager of International Mercantile Marine refused to believe the reports, saying: 'We place absolute confidence in the *Titanic*. We believe that the boat is unsinkable.' By the following morning, 16 April, the disaster was all over the news and the White Star office in New York was besieged by family and friends of the *Titanic*'s passengers. Many were furious and wanted answers from White Star, who had claimed that the ship could not sink.

American politician William Alden Smith demanded an immediate inquiry, while the survivors could still remember clearly what had happened. Just five days after the ship went down, the US Senate launched its investigation, which lasted 18 days. A couple of weeks later, the British Board of Trade began its own inquiry. It wanted to learn more about the safety of the ship, and whether passengers in steerage had been prevented from getting into the lifeboats (they had not, the inquiry found).

Safely does it

The US inquiry into the sinking led to major changes in international laws to improve safety at sea:

- In future there had to be enough lifeboats and lifejackets for all on board, and regular emergency drills.
- Crews would be properly trained to lower lifeboats and practise handling and rowing them. Ships must have at least two searchlights.
- Every ship had to have a radio operator on duty 24 hours a day.
- Ships must cross the Atlantic 60 miles (100 km) further south when there was an increased risk of icebergs.
- An International Ice Patrol was created in February 1914. Two ships would patrol regular routes across the Atlantic to warn of any possible ice hazards. Icebergs would be tracked as they approached shipping lanes, and there would be wider reporting of ice by all ships in the area. The Ice Patrol is still around today, helped by hi-tech equipment such as drift buoys that send back data about the water temperature and current via satellite. It has certainly been a success: no lives have been lost due to icebergs in the North Atlantic since the *Titanic* went down.

Remembering the heroes...

The US inquiry awarded a gold medal to Captain Arthur Rostron of the *Carpathia* on behalf of the American people, while the *Titanic* survivors clubbed together to buy a silver cup for the captain and 320 medals for his crew. The cup was presented to Captain Rostron by Mrs Molly Brown.

Captain Rostron had a long and distinguished career in command of troop ships and civilian liners, and was knighted in 1926.

...and the victims

Every year, on the anniversary of the sinking, a Lockheed C-130 Hercules aircraft of the International Ice Patrol flies over the wreck site and drops a wreath in tribute to the victims of the disaster.

Both reports blamed the disaster on the lack of proper lookouts, on the decision to steam at full speed through ice-infested waters, and the fact that the lifeboats weren't properly manned. They also found that the *Californian* and her captain, Stanley Lord, could have done a lot more to save those on the *Titanic*.

What had been learned? As well as creating new safety laws, the inquiries recommended better watertight compartments, lifeboats for all, and regular eye tests for lookouts. That said, the British inquiry was something of a whitewash. It let White Star off the hook as it didn't want passengers to switch to rival French or German firms. The Board of Trade also quietly ignored the fact that it had passed the *Titanic* as fit for sea in the first place.

You would have though that the fate of the *Titanic* would make people think twice about building giant vessels. No sirree! At 269 m long, the *Titanic* would have been dwarfed by some of today's superliners, such as the *Oasis of the Seas*, built in 2009, which is a whopping 362 m – almost as long as four football pitches.

Whodunnit?

Was anyone to blame for the tragedy?

- **Captain Smith**, for not taking the ice warnings seriously? It does seem it bit odd that he went to bed during the most hazardous part of the voyage, knowing full well that his ship was steaming into an area where icebergs had been spotted by several other ships. He was probably just overconfident about his ship – passenger Elmer Taylor heard him boasting that the ship could be cut in thirds and still stay afloat.

- **J. Bruce Ismay**, accused of persuading Captain Smith to plough on at full speed? Though the US Senate found him not guilty, witnesses such as Emily Ryerson and Elizabeth Lines were both convinced that Ismay wanted the ship to speed up, and had encouraged Captain Smith (who worked for him) to go faster.

  Some argue that Ismay's dream of a giant ship did cause problems. The *Olympic*-class ships were so much bigger than those before that accidents were more likely, such as the near miss with the *New York* in Southampton and the *Olympic*'s collision with HMS *Hawke*. *Olympic* had also crunched the rear end of a tug in New York in 1911 as she reversed her engines. The sheer size of the *Titanic* also meant that when she hit the iceberg she didn't bounce off but kept grinding against it.

- **Thomas Andrews**, the designer, for not making the ship safer? In Andrews's defence, *Titanic* was one of the safest ships of her time. No-one thought about the possibility of an iceberg scraping along the side – it just hadn't happened before.

- **First Officer Murdoch**, who ordered the engines to be stopped? The faster a ship goes, the faster it can turn. So if she had kept going at full speed, she just might have missed the iceberg completely. Alternatively, if the *Titanic* had crashed straight into the iceberg, it's likely that fewer compartments would have been flooded and most of the passengers would have survived.[7]

- **Quartermaster Robert Hichens**, for making a wrong turn? In 2010, Second Officer Charles Lightoller's granddaughter claimed Hichens was the real culprit. In those days, many sailors were accustomed to sailing with a tiller, which you push the opposite way to the direction you want to go. Lightoller admitted to his wife that Hichens got confused, as the *Titanic*'s steering wheel worked like that on a car, where you turn it in the direction you want to go. If you believe this story, Hichens steered the ship straight into the iceberg.

7. In 1879 the record-breaking British passenger liner SS Arizona *stayed afloat after hitting an iceberg head-on off the coast of Newfoundland. Though her bow was completely crushed, she limped back to St John's, Newfoundland, where repairs were carried out before she returned to Scotland.*

- **The lookouts**, who should have been using binoculars? It later emerged that there was a pair of binoculars on board the vessel, but no-one knew they were there. Given the conditions, however, they might not have made much difference, and you can't really blame the lookouts for not spotting something that was so hard to see.

- **The wireless operators**, who failed to deliver an important ice warning? At 9.30 p.m. on the night of the disaster, the steamer *Mesaba* warned of 'heavy pack ice and great number large icebergs'. Had Captain Smith read this, he would have been in no doubt about the dangers ahead. Again, you can't blame the overworked wireless team too much, as they were probably exhausted after spending 6 hours the night before repairing their broken set. They were also under a great deal of pressure to transmit the backlog of messages from passengers.

- **White Star**, for not providing enough lifeboats? The White Star Line certainly deserved criticism for its boastful claims of safety. But even if there had been more lifeboats, there probably wasn't enough time to launch them. Nonetheless, the crew on the *Titanic* should have been better trained for emergencies. Remember too that the *Titanic* was only half full (1,300 or so passengers out of a possible 2,603), so the loss could have been much worse.

- **Harland and Wolff**, for a bad job of building the Titanic? It has been claimed that the rivets used to hold the plates together weren't up to scratch and popped out too easily when the iceberg scraped along the side of the ship. Yet the *Olympic*, built using the same methods, was nicknamed the 'Old Reliable' and served for another 23 years. She's also the only merchant ship known to have rammed and sunk a German submarine!

- **Captain Lord** of the *Californian*, who should have come to the rescue? After a century of heated debate, they jury is still out on this one. An official report in 1992 concluded that the *Californian* should have investigated the white distress rockets fired by the *Titanic*. And why didn't Captain Lord wake his radio operator to check for any distress calls? Some experts claim that even if Lord had rushed to the scene, the *Californian* would have arrived just a few minutes before the *Titanic* sank. So, though he might have saved a few hundred people, over a thousand would still have died.

Or was it just a freak accident? Out of more than 30,000 transatlantic crossings in the previous 20 years, there were only 25 incidents in which ships or lives were lost – and the total number of deaths came to just 148, including passengers and crew.

Tight-fisted

If the White Star Line felt any guilt about what had happened, they certainly didn't show it in their financial dealings with the victims and survivors.

- Most of the crew had signed on just a few days before sailing. As they weren't considered permanent staff, White Star didn't offer their families any compensation.[8]

- The wages of the 212 surviving crew members were only paid up to the exact moment when the ship sank.

- White Star even asked the families of the orchestra on the *Titanic* to repay them five shillings and fourpence (approx. 27p) to cover the loss of their uniforms.

- It took 3½ years of legal action before White Star paid out $664,000 to settle all claims arising from the sinking of the *Titanic*, including:

  - $50 to Eugene Daly for a set of bagpipes
  - $750 to Robert Daniel for his champion bulldog
  - $5,000 to William Carter for his Renault car.

8. However, the British Titanic Relief Fund raised £450,000 for the hardest-hit families of victims.

Goldmine or graveyard?

After the sinking, there were rumours that the *Titanic* had been carrying a fortune in gold bullion.[9] This is almost certainly a myth, but the many millionaires on board must have left behind a treasure trove of valuable jewellery. Not surprisingly, for decades people dreamt of raising the ship to the surface, but until the 1980s there just wasn't the technology to find a ship nearly 4 km down on the seabed.

Finally, in 1985, US scientist Robert Ballard and French engineer Jean-Louis Michel teamed up to locate the wreck. Their first attempt ended in failure as bad weather forced them to call off the search. A couple of weeks later they returned in a new vessel, the *Knorr*, which carried two robot submersibles. These could take pictures and relay them back to the surface. Again, the team failed to find anything for 10 days. Then Ballard decided to look for debris from the wreck, which was likely to be spread out over a much wider area.

9. One of the first serious salvage efforts was prompted by claims that the ship carried a cargo of $100 million in gold and silver.

Early on 1 September 1985, the underwater camera on the submersible *Argo* sent up a picture of one of the *Titanic*'s giant boilers. Eureka! Soon after, the bow section of the ship was discovered and for the first time it was confirmed that the *Titanic* had broken into two pieces. The following year, Ballard dived down in a tiny three-person sub called *Alvin*. Incredibly, he was able to look inside the wreck by steering into the giant hole left by a collapsing funnel. A tiny robot, known as *Jason Jr.*, was deployed to explore deeper inside the ship. Ballard's team later found the *Titanic*'s stern, about 600 metres away from the bow. There wasn't that much left of it – the great steel hull had been ripped apart as it imploded on its way down to the bottom – and the wreck was now home to crabs, starfish and deep-sea fish.

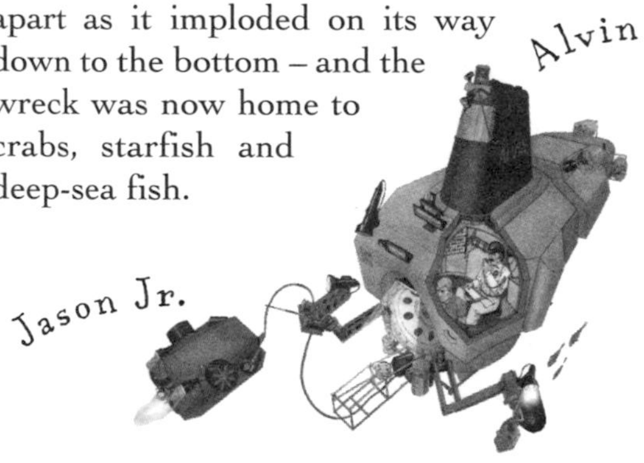

Alvin

Jason Jr.

A secret mission

The truth behind Robert Ballard's expedition to find the *Titanic* was only made public in October 2010. In 1985, Ballard was secretly working with the US Navy in a search for two nuclear submarines, USS *Thresher* and *Scorpion*, which had sunk in the North Atlantic. The Navy wanted to know what had happened to the nuclear reactors on board, and whether the *Scorpion* had been sunk by the Soviet Navy (probably not). Only once Ballard had completed his mission was he given permission to use the Navy's submersibles to hunt for the *Titanic*.

Once Ballard had realised his dream of finding the *Titanic*, he wanted the ghostly ship and her victims to be left undisturbed. He took nothing from the site, and left a plaque asking other explorers to do the same. Ballard's plea was ignored, and over the past 25 years salvage teams have recovered over 5,500 objects from the wreck. These have been sold to private collectors and exhibited in museums all over the world, where they have been seen by over 20 million people.

The debate still rages over whether the wreck should be left alone. The main two sections will probably stay put – they're just too massive to bring to the surface.[10] An expedition in September 2010 investigated how long it would take for the ship to fall apart. A pair of robots took thousands of photos and hours of video footage of the famous shipwreck, which revealed that the old ship is not rusting away as quickly as some experts had predicted.[11]

Cutlery, crockery, shoes and even a clarinet have been brought to the surface, yet many people feel that the 1,495 or so souls who went down with the ship should be left in peace. That won't happen. People are just too fascinated by the story of the *Titanic,* a detective mystery on an epic scale. We will never know the whole truth about what happened – it's buried deep in the dark, silent waters at the bottom of the Atlantic Ocean.

10. In 1998, however, a French team did manage to raise a section of the hull, known as the 'Big Piece'.
11. The hull is already covered in a carpet of 'rusticles'. These long fingers of rust are formed as bacteria eat away at the iron hull. Meanwhile, wood-boring molluscs have already eaten most of the softer material, such as the carpets and the wooden decks and furniture.

What happened to the survivors?

- **Baby:** Millvina Dean, the last remaining survivor, was nine weeks old in April 1912. After the *Titanic* was rediscovered in 1985 she became something of a celebrity: reporters interviewed her about her story and she was invited to open exhibitions about the *Titanic*. Miss Dean died in 2009, aged 97.

- **Toddlers:** Two-year-old Edmond Navratil and his elder brother Michel became known as the '*Titanic* orphans' as they were the only children rescued without a parent. (Their father, who had abducted them from his estranged wife, went down with the ship.) Their mother sailed to New York to collect them and return them to France. Michel eventually became a professor of psychology. In 1996 he joined fellow survivors on a cruise to the site of the wreck. The last male survivor of the *Titanic*, he died in 2001.

- **Child:** Like many of the survivors, 12-year-old Ruth Becker refused to talk about the sinking for many years. She later became a teacher. In March 1990 she went on her first sea cruise since 1912, and she died later that year. Four years later, her ashes were sprinkled over the very spot where the *Titanic* had sunk 82 years before.

- **Millionairess:** 19-year-old Madeleine Astor gave birth to J. J. Astor's son in August 1912. Though she would have been allowed to keep Astor's millions if she had stayed single, she remarried during the First World War. She died in 1947.

- **Sportsman:** The injuries that R. Norris Williams suffered during the sinking were so bad that doctors wanted to amputate his legs. But Williams refused, and by the end of the year he was ranked the No. 2 tennis player in America. He was one of a handful of survivors who used their return ticket back to Europe. Williams later won the Davis Cup with fellow survivor Karl Behr, and won a gold medal for tennis in the 1924 Olympics. He died in 1968.

- **Owner:** J. Bruce Ismay's reputation was badly damaged after surviving the disaster, and he left his job as managing director of the White Star Line in 1913. Always a private man, he saw very few people in the later years of his life and no-one was allowed to mention the *Titanic* in his presence (though he liked to read the shipping news). He died in 1937.

- **Officer:** Second Officer Charles Lightoller became a commander in the Royal Navy in the First World War, before turning his hand to chicken farming. In the Second World War he sailed his yacht as part of the armada of small boats that brought British soldiers home across the English Channel from Dunkirk. He died in 1952.

- **Hero:** Captain Arthur Rostron of the *Carpathia* served in the merchant navy during the First World War and eventually became Commodore of the entire Cunard Fleet in 1938. He died in 1940.

- **Sister ships:** The *Olympic* was given a hasty refit in late 1912, including the addition of 48 lifeboats. She served as a troop ship throughout the First World War and made her last Atlantic crossing in March 1935.

  The *Britannic*, launched in February 1914, was commandeered by the Royal Navy to serve as a hospital ship in the Mediterranean. She was struck by a mine or a torpedo on 21 November 1916 and went down with the loss of 30 lives. Even though her hull had been reinforced after the *Titanic* disaster, the *Britannic* sank in less than an hour.

Last but not least:

- **Serial survivor:** Stewardess Violet Jessop was on board the *Olympic* when it collided with HMS *Hawke* in 1911. The following year she survived the sinking of the *Titanic*. In 1916 she was a nurse on board the *Britannic* when it blew up. She jumped out of a lifeboat to avoid being sucked into the propellers, and banged her head on the giant keel before being picked up by another lifeboat. She died in 1971, aged 83.

Ten *Titanic* myths

1. **Claim:** The *Titanic* was switched with her sister ship *Olympic* as part of an insurance scam. The so-called *Titanic* didn't hit an iceberg, but collided with one of the ships waiting in the darkness to take passengers on board after the liner was scuttled.

   Verdict: It's hard to believe that any of the ship's officers would have gone along with such a plan.

2. **Claim:** Several men sneaked into the *Titanic*'s lifeboats by dressing as women.

   Verdict: Partly true. Edward Ryan admitted in a letter to his parents that he had put a shawl over his head to pass as a woman. But other stories were made up. For example, stockbroker William T. Sloper was accused of disguising himself by a New York newspaper, probably out of spite because he gave an exclusive to a local paper based in his home town. The poor man eventually had to put up a large fence around his family estate to stop people prying.

3. **Claim:** The *Titanic* sank because it was cursed by an Egyptian mummy carried on board.

   Verdict: False. The British Museum does have a coffin cover which has been said to be unlucky. It belonged to the so-called priestess of Amun-Ra. But it never left the museum until 1990. The myth arose because passenger William Stead (see page 47) loved to spook other travellers on board the *Titanic* with his tale of the cursed mummy.

4. **Claim:** The *Titanic* was actually sunk by an explosion.

   Verdict: False. Lady Duff Gordon wrote in her account of the sinking: 'The boat's stern lifted in the air and there was a tremendous explosion.' Others have suggested that the ship sank due to an explosion caused when ice-cold water pouring into the ship hit the hot coals in the fireboxes. But the evidence from other eye-witnesses and the wreck itself does not seem to support either theory.

5. **Claim:** The *Titanic*'s safes were carrying a fortune in jewellery when the ship went down.

   Verdict: True – there were a lot of very wealthy people aboard. Though it's unlikely that the *Titanic* carried gold bullion (see page 161), another White Star ship certainly did. The *Laurentic*, which sank off the coast of Northern Ireland in 1917 after hitting a mine, was carrying 36 tonnes of gold ingots. Remarkably, 3,186 gold bars out of 3,211 had been recovered by British Navy divers by 1924. Some 20 bars are still at the bottom of Lough Swilly!

6. **Claim:** One female passenger divorced her husband for deserting her.

Verdict: True – at least, so she claimed. In 1914, Mrs Lucile Carter complained that her husband had abandoned his wife and children, backing up her claim with the findings of the British inquiry which stated that her husband's lifeboat had departed 15 minutes earlier than theirs (Lifeboat No. 4). She was probably just looking for an excuse to divorce him, as recent research suggests his lifeboat, Collapsible C, actually left later. So his story that he accompanied his wife, her maid and his children to Lifeboat No. 4 may have been true.

7. **Claim:** Fireman Frank Tower survived the sinkings of the *Titanic* (1912), the *Empress of Ireland* (1914) and the *Lusitania* (1915).

Verdict: False. No person by the name of Frank Tower appears in any crew lists for these three vessels.

8. **Claim:** *Titanic*'s hull number, 390904, spells out 'No Pope' when seen in a mirror:

3909 04 NO POPE

Verdict: False. This is probably just pub talk stemming from Belfast's rival Protestant and Catholic communities.

Titanic's hull number was 401 and her Board of Trade number 131428.

9. **Claim:** Workers were trapped in the hull while the ship was being built.

   Verdict: False. This tall tale is borrowed from a myth about an earlier liner, the *Great Eastern*. While she was being built, boys worked in the narrow space between the double skins of the *Great Eastern*'s hull. Later, the sounds of hammering below decks were blamed on the ghosts of boys trapped in the hull.

10. **Claim:** Irish passengers in steerage suffered more than other nationalities.

    Verdict: False. There were 113 Irish people in third class (out of 708), and 40 (or 35.4 per cent) were saved. In fact, the Irish fared better than many other nationalities in third class, such as the Americans (28 per cent survived) and British (just 15 per cent of whom survived).

Titanic tourist sites

- **Belfast, Northern Ireland.** In Belfast's '*Titanic* Quarter', guided boat tours take in the Harland & Wolff shipyards, including the famous Thompson dock where the *Titanic* was built, and the *Titanic* Drawing Rooms (right) where the designs were drawn up. A new *Titanic* exhibition opened on 31 May 2011 at the Ulster Folk and Transport Museum. At the Northern Ireland Science Park you can also visit SS *Nomadic*, tender ship to the *Titanic* and the only surviving White Star Line boat. In the town of Comber, east of Belfast, there's a memorial hall opened in January 1914 to remember the

Titanic's main architect, Thomas Andrews. You can even buy a T-shirt giving Belfast's take on the disaster: 'She was alright when she left here!'

- **Southampton, England.** Home to several grave sites (such as the Old Cemetery) of *Titanic* victims, as well as the excellent Southampton Maritime Museum. The new Sea City Museum, part of which is dedicated to the story of the *Titanic*, opens in 2012. There is a memorial in the Ocean Dock to the victims, though you can't see Berth 44 (from which *Titanic* sailed) without special permission. Another memorial at the Holyrood Church on the High Street is dedicated to the firemen, stewards and crew from Southampton who went down with the ship. Several first-class passengers, including Bruce Ismay and Thomas Andrews, stayed at the Southwestern Hotel (still standing) on Canute Street the night before the *Titanic* sailed.

- **Halifax, Nova Scotia, Canada.** One hundred and fifty *Titanic* victims were buried in Halifax, and visitors can explore the Mount Olivet and Fairlawn Cemeteries where the *Titanic* graves are marked by a display. There is also an exhibition on the *Titanic* in Halifax's Maritime Museum of the Atlantic, including artefacts such as a deck chair pulled from the water in the weeks after the sinking.

- **Indian Orchard, Massachusetts, USA.** The *Titanic* Museum here focuses on the survivors, and exhibits many personal items such as letters, postcards and menus.

- **Cobh, Ireland** (formerly Queenstown). There's a stone monument in Pearse Square with a plaque commemorating the *Titanic*. You can also see the building that housed the White Star Line offices, and the pier where passengers boarded the tenders to be ferried out to the ship.

- **Denver, Colorado, USA.** Here you can visit the home of famous *Titanic* survivor Molly Brown.

- **London, England.** The White Star Line's London offices, named Oceanic House, still exist today on Cockspur Street, just a short walk from Trafalgar Square.

- **Liverpool, England.** There is a gallery dedicated to the *Titanic* disaster at the Merseyside Maritime Museum.

- **New York City, USA.** Outside the South Street Seaport Museum you can see the *Titanic* Memorial, an 18-metre-high lighthouse built in 1913 with donations following a campaign supported by survivor Molly Brown. There is also a memorial statue to victims Isidor and Ida Straus at 106th Street and Broadway.

Titanic on film and stage

- **1912.** Shortly after the tragedy, a 10-minute newsreel was shown in movie theatres – but most of the footage actually showed the *Olympic*.

- **1912.** One survivor of the disaster, Dorothy Gibson, was a silent-screen actress, and just weeks after her rescue she starred in a movie about the *Titanic*, wearing a dress she wore on the night of the sinking. Sadly, no copies of the film survive.

- **1938.** Alfred Hitchcock almost directed a film about the *Titanic* but it was scrapped after the project went over budget. The producer, David O. Selznick, had planned to buy an old liner and rebuild the top decks to look like the *Titanic*.

- **1943.** During the Second World War the Nazis made a propaganda film about the disaster. But the film was pulled after they found that German audiences felt sorry for the British and American passengers.

- **1953.** Hollywood turned the story of the *Titanic* into a gripping melodrama starring Barbara Stanwyck, Clifton Webb and Robert Wagner. In one scene, Stanwyck got so upset thinking about the original disaster that she burst into tears and the whole crew had to wait until she recovered her composure.

- **1958.** Many experts regard *A Night to Remember* as the most accurate portrayal of the night of the sinking. Shot like a documentary, it starred Kenneth More as Second Officer Lightoller. The producer, William MacQuitty, had watched the launch of *Titanic* as a boy in Belfast in 1911. The sets were built from actual blueprints of *Titanic* and actors were chosen to look like the people they portrayed.

- **1964.** In 1960 a musical, *The Unsinkable Molly Brown*, had opened on Broadway, celebrating the life of the famous *Titanic* survivor. Four years later it was made into a movie starring Debbie Reynolds, who was nominated for an Oscar.

- **1980.** The movie *Raise the Titanic* was based on a bestselling novel by Clive Cussler. Its plot centred around an attempt by the US Navy to raise the liner; its cargo hold allegedly contained a rare mineral called byzanium, needed for a nuclear defence system. The film was a flop, even though the special effects alone cost more than it did to build the *Titanic* itself in 1911!

- **1981.** Fantasy film *Time Bandits* followed a group of time-travelling dwarves who, among other adventures, end up on the deck of the *Titanic*.

- **1997.** The story was again given the blockbuster treatment; though 1997's *Titanic* cost $200 million to make, it became one of the most successful movies of all time. Directed by James Cameron, the film starred Kate Winslet and Leonardo Di Caprio as two fictional passengers. During filming, Winslet said she was afraid of drowning in the giant water tank in which the ship was to be sunk.

  Cameron made several dives to see the sunken liner for himself. Many of the props and fittings on the film set – from the chandeliers to the lifeboat davits – were constructed by the same firms that had worked on the original ship.

A *Titanic* recipe

Why not try making one of the desserts enjoyed by second-class passengers aboard the *Titanic*?

Coconut sandwich

Ingredients

- ½ cup butter, softened
- ½ cup granulated sugar
- ½ tsp. vanilla extract
- 1 egg
- 1 cup plain flour
- ⅔ cup sweetened shredded coconut
- ¼ teaspoon freshly grated nutmeg
- 1 egg white, beaten

For the cream filling:

- 1 tbsp. vegetable oil
- 1 tbsp. butter
- ¾ cup icing sugar
- 1 tbsp. shredded coconut
- Dash pure vanilla extract

Method

1. Using an electric mixer, cream the butter until light, then add granulated sugar and continue beating at a medium speed for 5 minutes until light and fluffy.

2. Add vanilla extract and egg, and beat until fully mixed.
3. On a low speed, mix in the flour, coconut and nutmeg until blended.
4. Shape into a dough ball and refrigerate for 1–2 hours.
5. Divide the dough into two portions and roll out each half to 5 mm thick. Cut into circles using a pastry cutter, and carefully place on a greased baking sheet, using a spatula.
6. Lightly brush each piece of cut dough with beaten egg white. Bake at 180°C for 8 to 10 minutes or until golden-brown on the base.
7. Place the wafers on a cooling rack and allow them to cool completely.

Cream filling

8. Cream together the oil and butter, adding icing sugar gradually until creamy. Stir in the coconut and vanilla.
9. Spread the filling evenly over half the wafers and top with the remaining wafers to make sandwiches.
10. Invite your friends over for a *Titanic* treat!

Titanic tunes

The Roast Beef of Old England

These are the words to the tune played by the Titanic's *bugler, P. W. Fletcher, to call first-class passengers to meals:*

When mighty roast beef was the Englishman's
  food,
It ennobled our hearts, and enriched our
  blood,
Our soldiers were brave, and our courtiers
  were good,
O! the Roast Beef of Old England!
And O! for old England's Roast Beef!

Our fathers of old were robust, stout and
  strong,
And kept open house, with good cheer all day
  long,
Which made their plump tenants rejoice in this
  song –
O! the Roast Beef of Old England!
And O! for old England's Roast Beef!

When good Queen Elizabeth sat on the throne,
Ere coffee, or tea, or such slip-slops were
  known,
The world was in terror if e'er she did frown.
O! the Roast Beef of Old England!
And O! for old England's Roast Beef!

Richard Leveridge (1670–1758)

Nearer, my God, to Thee

According to some passengers, this hymn was the last tune played by the Titanic*'s eight-man orchestra just before the ship went down:*

Nearer, my God, to thee, nearer to thee!
E'en though it be a cross that raiseth me,
Still all my song shall be,
Nearer, my God, to thee;
Nearer, my God, to thee, nearer to thee!

Though like the wanderer, the sun gone down,
Darkness be over me, my rest a stone;
Yet in my dreams I'd be
Nearer, my God, to thee;
Nearer, my God, to thee, nearer to thee!

There let the way appear, steps unto Heaven;
All that thou sendest me, in mercy given;
Angels to beckon me
Nearer, my God, to thee;
Nearer, my God, to thee, nearer to thee!

Then, with my waking thoughts bright with
thy praise,
Out of my stony griefs Bethel I'll raise;
So by my woes to be
Nearer, my God, to thee;
Nearer, my God, to thee, nearer to thee!

Or if, on joyful wing cleaving the sky,
Sun, moon, and stars forgot, upward I fly,
Still all my song shall be,
Nearer, my God, to thee;
Nearer, my God, to thee, nearer to thee!

Sarah F. Adams (1805–1848)

Glossary

aft Towards the stern (back) of a ship.

berth A bed or bunk inside a ship; also, a place where a ship docks.

Blue Peter A blue flag with a white square in the middle. It is hoisted when a ship is about to sail.

boat deck The upper deck, where lifeboats are stored.

bosun's chair A seat consisting of a plank hanging from ropes.

bow The front of a ship.

bridge The control room from which the captain or commander of a ship gives instructions.

bulkhead A wall dividing the hull of a ship into sections. The *Titanic*'s bulkheads were designed to form watertight compartments in the event of a leak.

collapsible lifeboat (or **Engelhardt**) A lifeboat with canvas sides that could be folded flat for easy storage.

crow's nest A lookout platform high up a ship's mast.

davit A crane for launching boats.

displacement A measure of the mass of a ship.

dry dock A large dock from which water can be pumped out; it is used for building ships, or for repairing a ship below its waterline.

emigrant A person who leaves their country to begin a new life in another.

fireman Another name for a stoker, a worker who shovels coal into a ship's boilers.

gangway A passageway into a ship.

gantry A tall framework of steel, fitted with cranes, used for working on the outside of a large structure.

graving dock Another name for a dry dock.

great circle A circle whose centre of radius is the centre of the earth.
knot A unit of speed used for ships. One knot is one nautical mile per hour, equivalent to 1.85 km/h.
liner A ship that sails on fixed routes, or 'lines'.
maiden voyage A ship's first journey.
manifest An inventory (detailed list) of a ship's cargo.
Morse code A telegraph code using a system of 'dots and dashes' (short and long sounds or flashes of light) for letters.
port The left-hand side of a ship (where ships once tied up to avoid damaging the steerboard, or rudder).
porthole A small round window in the side of a ship.
Provincial A senior member of certain religious orders.
purser The officer responsible for money on board a ship.
rivet A metal pin used to hold metal plates together.
RMS Royal Mail Steamer.
sea trials Tests carried out to see whether a new ship is fit to go to sea.
shipping line A company that owns a fleet of ships.
sister ship A ship that is built to the same design as another (though there may be small differences).
starboard The right-hand side of a ship (where the *steerboard* or rudder once was).
stateroom A first-class cabin.
steerage The cheapest accommodation on a ship, usually on the lowest decks.
stern The back end of a ship.
tender A small ship or boat used to ferry passengers and crew to a larger vessel.
waterline The level to which water rises up the hull of a ship when she is afloat.

Titanic timeline

Summer 1907 Lord Pirrie and J. Bruce Ismay first decide to build *Titanic* and her two sister ships.
29 July 1908 The design for *Titanic* is approved.
31 March 1909 *Titanic*'s keel is laid down in Belfast.
31 May 1911 The hull of the *Titanic* is launched.
31 March 1912 Fitting-out of *Titanic* is completed.
2 April 1912 *Titanic* passes her sea trials and leaves Belfast for Southampton that evening.
3 April 1912 *Titanic* arrives in Southampton. Over the next week, supplies, cargo and coal are loaded aboard.
6 April 1912 Majority of *Titanic*'s crew are recruited.

The maiden voyage

Wednesday 10 April 1912
5–7.30 a.m. Captain Smith and his crew go aboard.
9.30–11.30 a.m. Boat trains arrive. Passengers board.
12.00 noon *Titanic* sets sail from Southampton,almost crashing into the *New York* on the River Test.
5.30 p.m. *Titanic* arrives in Cherbourg, France.
8.10 p.m. *Titanic* leaves Cherbourg.

Thursday 11 April 1912
11.30 a.m. *Titanic* drops anchor off Queenstown.
1.55 p.m. *Titanic* sets sail across the Atlantic Ocean.

Friday 12 April 1912
12.00 noon By now, *Titanic* has covered 623 km.

Saturday 13 April 1912
12.00 noon Fine weather continues. *Titanic* has travelled another 835 km. First warning of heavy ice.

Sunday 14 April 1912
12.00 noon *Titanic* has sailed another 879 km.

5.50 p.m. After further ice warnings, Captain Smith alters course to avoid the ice field.

11.40 p.m Lookout Frederick Fleet spots an iceberg dead ahead. The iceberg strikes the starboard bow below the waterline. *Titanic* begins to take on water.

Monday 15 April 1912

12.05 a.m. Ship's designer Thomas Andrews estimates that *Titanic* will sink in under two hours.

12.45 a.m. First lifeboat is safely lowered.

12.55 a.m. The first of eight distress rockets is fired.

1.15 a.m. *Titanic*'s stern begins to rise out of the water.

1.30 a.m. Tables and chairs begin to slide down the deck. Passengers start to panic.

2.05 a.m. The last lifeboat is launched. There are still 1,500 people on board *Titanic*.

2.17 a.m. The last radio message is sent.

2.18 a.m. The ship's lights go out. *Titanic* breaks in two and the bow half sinks.

2.20 a.m. *Titanic*'s stern half tilts vertically then sinks.

3.00 a.m. By now, those in the water have frozen to death.

4.10 a.m. *Carpathia* begins picking up survivors.

8.50 a.m. *Carpathia* leaves for New York, carrying 705 survivors.

Wednesday 17 April 1912 White Star charters *Mackay-Bennett* to recover dead bodies.

Thursday 18 April 1912 *Carpathia* reaches New York.

The aftermath

19 April – 25 May 1912 US Senate inquiry.

2 May – 3 July 1912 British Board of Trade inquiry.

1 September 1985 Dr Robert Ballard discovers the wreck of the *Titanic*.

Index

T

W

Other Cherished  Library titles

Very Peculiar Histories™

Ancient Egypt
Mummy Myth and Magic
Jim Pipe
ISBN: 978-1-906714-92-5

The Blitz
David Arscott
ISBN: 978-1-907184-18-5

Brighton
David Arscott
ISBN: 978-1-906714-89-5

Castles
Jacqueline Morley
ISBN: 978-1-907184-48-2

Christmas
Fiona Macdonald
ISBN: 978-1-907184-50-5

Global Warming
Ian Graham
ISBN: 978-1-907184-51-2

Golf
David Arscott
ISBN: 978-1-907184-75-8

Great Britons
Ian Graham
ISBN: 978-1-907184-59-8

Ireland
Jim Pipe
ISBN: 978-1-905638-98-7

Kings & Queens
Antony Mason
ISBN: 978-1-906714-77-2

London
Jim Pipe
ISBN: 978-1-907184-26-0

The Olympics
David Arscott
ISBN: 978-1-907184-78-9

Rations
David Arscott
ISBN: 978-1-907184-25-3

Royal Weddings
Fiona Macdonald
ISBN: 978-1-907184-84-0

Other Cherished Library titles

Scotland

Fiona Macdonald

Vol. 1: From ancient times to Robert the Bruce

ISBN: 978-1-906370-91-6

Vol. 2: From the Stewarts to modern Scotland

ISBN: 978-1-906714-79-6

The Tudors

Jim Pipe

ISBN: 978-1-907184-58-1

Vampires

Fiona Macdonald

ISBN: 978-1-907184-39-0

Victorian Servants

Fiona Macdonald

ISBN: 978-1-907184-49-9

Wales

Rupert Matthews

ISBN: 978-1-907184-19-2

Whisky

Fiona Macdonald

ISBN: 978-1-907184-76-5

The World Cup

David Arscott

ISBN: 978-1-907184-38-3

World War One

Jim Pipe

ISBN: 978-1-908177-00-1

Yorkshire

John Malam

ISBN: 978-1-907184-57-4

Myths and Legends

Heroes, Gods and Monsters of

Ancient Greek Mythology

Michael Ford

ISBN: 978-1-906370-92-3

Heroes, Gods and Monsters of

Celtic Mythology

Fiona Macdonald

ISBN: 978-1-905638-97-0

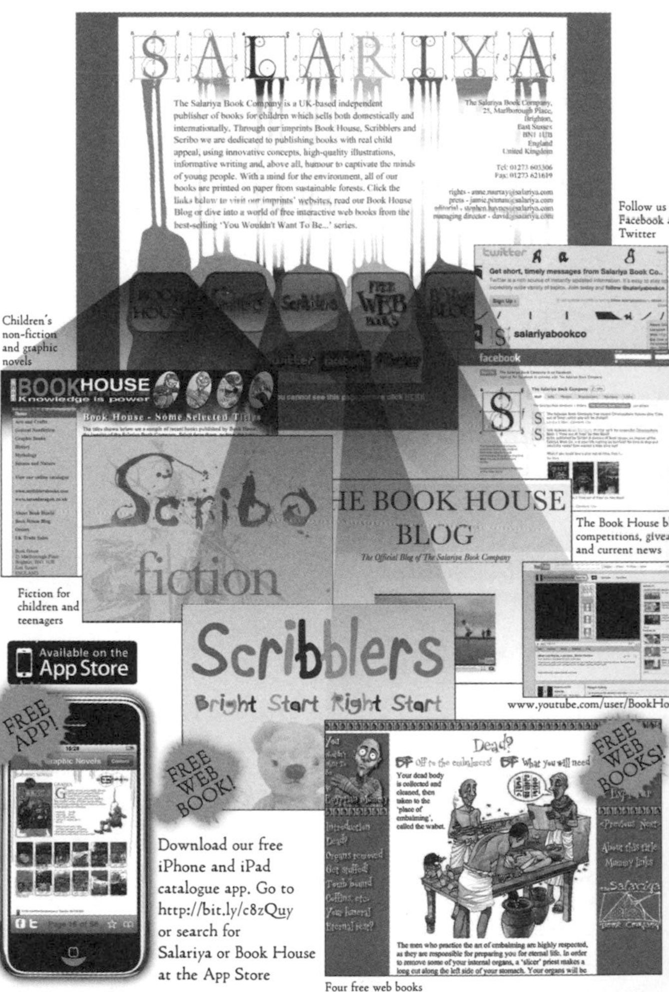
SALARIYA
The Salariya Book Company is a UK-based independent publisher of books for children which sells both domestically and internationally. Through our imprints Book House, Scribblers and Scribo we are dedicated to publishing books with real child appeal, using innovative concepts, high-quality illustrations, informative writing and, above all, humour to captivate the minds of young people. With a mind for the environment, all of our books are printed on paper from sustainable forests. Click the links below to visit our imprints' websites, read our Book House Blog or dive into a world of free interactive web books from the best-selling 'You Wouldn't Want To Be...' series.
Follow us on Facebook and Twitter
Children's non-fiction and graphic novels
BOOKHOUSE
Knowledge is power
Scribo fiction
Fiction for children and teenagers
THE BOOK HOUSE BLOG
The Official Blog of The Salariya Book Company
The Book House blog competitions, giveaways and current news
Scribblers
Bright Start Right Start
www.youtube.com/user/BookHou
Available on the App Store
FREE APP!
FREE WEB BOOK!
FREE WEB BOOKS!
Dead?
Download our free iPhone and iPad catalogue app. Go to http://bit.ly/c8zQuy or search for Salariya or Book House at the App Store
Four free web books